THE APOSTOLIC CHURCH

The Apostolic Church

THOMAS WITHEROW

FREE PRESBYTERIAN PUBLICATIONS

FREE PRESBYTERIAN PUBLICATIONS
133 Woodlands Road
Glasgow
G3 6LE

First published 1856

First FPP edition 1954
(reprinted from the fifth edition of 1881)

Sixth printing, completely reset, 1990

Reprinted 1997, 2001, 2003

This edition © Free Presbyterian Publications 1990

ISBN 0 902506 04 8

Typesetting by
Settle Graphics

Printed by
Pioneer Press Limited
Skipton
North Yorkshire
BD23 2TZ

Contents

CHAPTER ONE

Statement of the Question

IT IS VERY COMMON for professing Christians to draw a distinction between *essentials* and *non-essentials* in religion, and to infer that, if any fact or doctrine rightly belongs to the latter class, it must be a matter of very little importance, and may in practice be safely set at nought. The great bulk of men take their opinions on trust; they will not undergo the toil of thinking, searching, and reasoning about anything, and one of the most usual expedients adopted to save them the trouble of inquiry, and to turn aside the force of any disagreeable fact, is to meet it by saying, "The matter is not essential to salvation; therefore we need give ourselves little concern on the subject."

If the distinction here specified is safe, the inference drawn from it is certainly dangerous. To say that, because a fact of Divine revelation is not essential to salvation, it must of necessity be unimportant, and may or may not be received by us, is to assert a principle, the application of which would make havoc of our Christianity. For, what are the truths essential to salvation? Are they not these: That there is a God; that all men are sinners; that the Son of God died upon the cross to make atonement for the guilty; and that whosoever believes on the Lord Jesus Christ shall be saved? There is good reason for believing that not a few souls are now in happiness, who in life knew little more than these — the first principles of the oracles of God — the very alphabet of the Christian system; and if so, no other Divine truths can be counted absolutely essential to salvation. But if all the other truths of revelation are unimportant, because they happen to be non-essentials, it follows that the Word of God itself is in the main unimportant; for by far the greatest portion of it is occupied with matters, the knowledge of which, in the case supposed, is not absolutely indispensable to the everlasting happiness of men. Nor does it alter the case, if we regard the number of fundamental truths to be much greater. Let a man once persuade himself that importance attaches only to what he is pleased to call essentials, whatever their number, and he will, no doubt, shorten his creed and cut away the foundation of many controversies; but he will practically set aside all except a very small part of the Scriptures. If such a principle does not mutilate the Bible, it stigmatises much of it as trivial. Revelation is all gold for preciousness and purity, but the very touch of such a principle would transmute the most of it into dross.

Though every statement in the Scripture cannot be regarded as absolutely essential to salvation, yet everything there is essential to some other wise and important end, else it would not find a place in the good Word of God. Human wisdom may be baffled in attempting to specify the design of every truth that forms a component part of Divine revelation, but eternity will show us that no portion of it is useless. All Scripture is profitable. A fact written therein may not be essential to human salvation, and yet it may be highly conducive to some other great and gracious purpose in the economy of God — it may be necessary for our personal comfort, for our guidance in life, or for our growth in holiness, and most certainly it is essential to the completeness of the system of Divine truth. The law of the Lord is perfect. Strike out of the Bible the truth that seems the most insignificant of all, and the law of the Lord would not be perfect any more. In architecture, the pinning that fills a crevice in the wall occupies a subordinate position, in comparison with the quoin*; but the builder lets us know that the one has an important purpose to serve as well as the other, and does its part to promote the stability and completeness of the house. In shipbuilding, the screws and bolts that gird the ship together are insignificant, as compared with the beams of oak and masts of pine, but they contribute their full share to the safety of the vessel and the security of the passenger. So in the Christian system, every fact, great or small, that God has been pleased to insert in the Bible is, by its very position, invested with importance, answers its end, and, though perhaps justly considered as non-essential to salvation, does not deserve to be accounted as worthless.

Every Divine truth is important, though it may be that all Divine truths are not of equal importance. The simplest statement of the Bible is a matter of more concern to an immortal being than the most sublime sentiment of mere human genius. The one carries with it what the other cannot show — the stamp of the

---

[* A cornerstone.]

approval of God. The one comes to us from heaven, the other savours of the earth. The one has for us a special interest, as forming a constituent portion of that Word which is a message from God to each individual man; the other is the production of a mind merely human, to which we and all our interests were alike unknown. Any truth merely human should weigh with us light as a feather in comparison with the most insignificant of the truths of God. The faith of a Christian should strive to reach and grasp everything that God has honoured with a place in that Word, the design of which is to be a light to our feet as we thread our way through this dark world. Besides, this, unlike every other book, is not doomed to perish. Heaven and earth may pass away, but the words of Christ shall not pass away. The seal of eternity is stamped on every verse of the Bible. This fact is enough of itself to make every line of it important.

With these observations we deem it right to introduce our exposition of ecclesiastical polity. Few would go so far as to assert that correct views on Church government are essential to salvation, and yet it is a subject whose importance it were folly to attempt to depreciate. The Holy Spirit, speaking in the Scriptures, treats of this theme. The Christian world has been divided in opinion about it ever since the Reformation. We cannot attach ourselves to any denomination of Christians without giving our influence either to truth or error on this very point; and the views we adopt upon this subject go far to colour our opinions on matters of Christian faith and practice. With such facts before us, though we may not regard the polity of the New Testament Church as essential to human salvation, we do not feel at liberty to undervalue its importance.

The various forms of Church government that we find existing at present in the Christian world may be classed under some one or other of these three heads: *Prelacy, Independency,* and *Presbytery.* We do not employ these terms in an offensive sense, but as being the best calculated to denote their respective systems. *Prelacy* is that form of Church government which is administered by archbishops, bishops, deans, archdeacons, and other ecclesiastical office-bearers depending on that hierarchy; and is such as we see exemplified in the Greek Church, the Church of Rome, and the Church of England. *Independency* is that form of Church government whose distinctive principle is, that each separate congregation is under Christ subject to no external jurisdiction whatever, but has within itself — in its office-bearers and members — all the materials of government; and is such as is at present in practical operation among Congregationalists and Baptists. *Presbytery* is that form of Church government which is dispensed by presbyters or elders, met in Session, Presbytery, Synod, or General Assembly; and is such as is presented in the several Presbyterian Churches of Ireland, Scotland, England, and America. These three forms of ecclesiastical polity are at this moment extensively prevalent in Christendom. Indeed, every other organisation, that any considerable body of

Christians has adopted, is only a modification or a mixture of some of the systems we have named.

A very brief examination enables us to see that these three systems differ very widely in their characteristic features. Not only so, but Prelacy, in all its main principles, is opposed to Presbytery; and Independency, in its main principles, is opposed to both. It follows that three forms, differing so very much, cannot all be right, and cannot of course have equal claims on the attachment and support of enlightened and conscientious men. It is self-evident, moreover, that the Word of God, the only rule of faith and practice, cannot approve of all; for, as the Word of God never contradicts itself, it cannot sanction contradictory systems. Some one of the three must be more in accordance with the will of God, as expressed in the Scriptures, than either of the others; and to know which of them is so, should be a subject of deep interest to every child of God. A Christian, of all men, is bound to be a lover of the truth; and we are warranted in supposing that, if a Christian could only see to which of these competing systems the Word of Truth bears witness, he would support it with all his might, and would lend no encouragement to the others. If a man, after he sees the difference, can hold what he knows to be merely human in the same estimation with what he knows to be Divine, let him bid farewell to his Christianity, and cease to pretend that he cherishes any attachment to the truth. The religion of the Lord Jesus, except we mistake its spirit far, binds all who receive it to prefer the true to the false, the right to the wrong, the good to the evil; and for us to be tempted by any consideration to hold them in equal reverence and render them equal support, is to fling one of the first requirements of Christianity away from us. The influence of a Christian is often very little in this world, but whatever it is, it is a talent, for which, like his time, his money, or his intellectual power, he is accountable to God, and that influence ought ever to be on the side of the truth, never against the truth.

Which, then, of the three forms of Church government prevalent throughout the world is it the duty of a Christian to select and to support?

This is a question of great importance. It is, besides, forced upon our consideration in every locality where a dissenting chapel lifts its front, and a church steeple tapers into air. And yet it must be admitted, that the majority of Christians contrive to pass through life without ever giving an hour's thought to this most interesting theme. Most people are content to let their ancestors choose a church for them, and every Sabbath walk to Divine worship in the footsteps of their great-grandfathers — they know not why, and care not wherefore. Some shrink from inquiry, lest it should turn out that the Church to which they are bound by ties of family, education, and habit, is destitute of all Scriptural authority, and lest they feel uncomfortable by having their convictions and their interests set at war. But the great reason why the spirit of inquiry is almost dead on this subject is, that the pulpit is silent, or nearly so, on ecclesiastical government. On this topic the trumpet gives not an uncertain sound, but commonly no sound whatever. There are, we are persuaded, few ministers in any denomination who could say to their people that, on this subject, "we have not shunned to declare to you the whole counsel of God". The people never having had their attention specially directed to those passages of Scripture where the principles of Church government are embodied, give no time or thought to the consideration of the subject. The result is, that vast masses of men and women live in utter ignorance, not only of the Scriptural facts bearing on the case, but even of their own denominational peculiarities; they are Prelatists, Independents, or Presbyterians by birth, not by conviction; they view all forms of Church government as equally true, which is the same thing as to count them equally worthless; they have no definite ideas on the subject; and thus, in absence of public instruction, they are, by the education of circumstances, prepared to fall in with any system or no system, as may best suit their private convenience or promote their worldly ambition. So it is that many who, in the judgment of charity, are Christians, regard the denomination with which birth or accident has connected them, either with a blind attachment or a sinful indifference; and, though rival systems of Church polity have their representatives in every village, they plod the weary way of life in happy unconcern about all such matters, and are never troubled with the question that the very sight of a church spire suggests to other men — *Which of these is true?*

Most people who withdraw from the communion of one Church to connect themselves with another, and thus exercise their right of choice between the various forms of ecclesiastical government, are induced to give their preference from motives such as should never influence an intelligent Christian. They are guided by feeling rather than by judgment. They do not first ascertain the leading principles of the denomination from its acknowledged standards, and then examine these principles in the light of the Word of God. The bulk of mankind are not intellectual enough to search for principles and weigh them. At least, they do not take the trouble, but are influenced in their choice, either by the authority of some great man, or the moral worth of some particular persons, or the piety and eloquence of some local minister — or perhaps by paltry pique, or petty gain, or love of the rank or fashion of the world, or by some other equally low and vulgar consideration. But to decide the rival claims of Prelacy, Independency, and Presbytery by any such tests as these, is absurd in the extreme. Try them by the authority of great men! There is not one of the three systems that could not present a long catalogue of distinguished men, who were its warm supporters till the last hour of life. Test them by moral worth! There is not one of them that could not present a goodly number of the excellent of the earth, waiting on its ministrations and reposing beneath its shadow. If we ask which of these systems provides able and pious ministers to instruct the people, we find a large number of such persons filling the pulpits of each of them; and if we examine further, we will find that not unfrequently there may be in the same town a minister who is an eloquent man and mighty in the Scriptures, who, all the week in the garden of the Lord, is active as the busy bee, and who, when Sabbath comes, dispenses the sweets of the Divine Word to admiring multitudes; while, in connection with the same denomination, there may be on the other side of the street some poor pitiful drone, who is doomed to hum to vacancy all the year round. Any such modes of testing ecclesiastical systems, however common, are unsure and unsafe.

To us it seems there is a much more satisfactory way of deciding upon the claims of those forms of Church government which obtain at present in the world — that is, to test their peculiar principles by the standard of the Word of God. That book is quite sufficient to point out the path of duty to the Christian in this as well as in all other matters, for it was intended by its Divine Author to be our guide in matters of practice as well as of faith. The Bible furnishes us with peculiar facilities for forming an opinion on this very point. It tells us of a Church that was organised in the world eighteen hundred years ago. The founders of that Church were apostles and prophets, acting by the authority of God. Every fact known with certainty about the original constitution of the Church is preserved in the Bible, everything preserved elsewhere is only hearsay and tradition. We read in Scripture very many facts that enable us to know with tolerable accuracy the history, doctrine, worship, and government of that Church which existed in apostolic days. The principles of government set up in a Church which was founded by inspired men, must have had, we are sure, the approbation of God. Corruptions in government, as well as in doctrine, sprang up at a very early period, but the Church in apostolic days was purer than it ever has been in subsequent times. The most obvious method, therefore, of arriving at the truth is to compare our modern systems of ecclesiastical government with the model presented in the Holy Scriptures. That which bears the closest resemblance to the Divine original is most likely itself to be Divine.

The warmest friends of existing ecclesiastical systems cannot fairly object to such a test. There is scarcely a Church on earth that is not loud in its pretentions to apostolicity. The Prelatic Churches claim to be apostolic. The Independent Churches claim to be apostolic. The Presbyterian Churches claim to be apostolic. Each of these denominations professes to maintain the same doctrine, worship, and government that distinguished the Church which was planted by the apostles of the Lord. On one of these points — that of ecclesiastical government — we propose to examine these claims by the very test that themselves have chosen. Divesting ourselves of all prejudice, we come to the law and to the testimony, desirous to know what God says on the topic in question, and determined to follow where the Scripture points, let that be where it may. Let us search the Bible, to see what it teaches on this great theme. If, on a thorough examination, we fail to discover there any clear and definite principles of Church government, the conclusion of necessity follows, that Prelacy, Independency, and Presbytery are upon a level — none of them is based upon Divine authority — and it becomes a matter of mere expediency or convenience which form we support. If we find, on the other hand, that certain great principles of Church government are embodied in the Scriptures, then, when we have ascertained accurately what these principles are, we have reached the mind of God upon the matter, and we have discovered a touch-stone, wherewith we can try the value of existing systems, and determine how much is human and how much Divine in every one of them.

MEANING OF THE WORD CHURCH

THE WORD *CHURCH* in our common discourse is used in a variety of senses. Sometimes it signifies the material building erected for Divine worship; sometimes it means the people usually assembling in such a building; sometimes the aggregate body of the clergy as distinguished from the laity; sometimes the collective body of professing Christians. As general use is the law of language, it does not become us to take exception to the variety of significations that are given to the term by our best writers; nor can we even say that much practical inconvenience arises from them, inasmuch as the accompanying circumstances usually determine the specific sense in which the word is to be understood. But it is never to be forgotten that, when we come to the interpretation of the Word of God, the variety of senses commonly attached to the term is altogether inadmissable, and would, if adopted, darken and corrupt the meaning of Divine revelation. The word Church in Scripture has always one meaning, and one only — *an assembly of the people of God — a society of Christians.* The Greek word *ecclesia,* in its primary and civil sense, means any assembly called together for any purpose (Acts 19:32); but in its appropriated and religious sense, it means *a society of Christians,* and is invariably translated by the word *Church.* Examine the Scriptures from the commencement to the close, and you find that the word Church never has any other meaning but that which we have stated. Let any man who feels disposed to dispute this statement, produce, if he can, any passage from the Word of God where the sense would be impaired, if the phrase *society of Christians,* or *Christian assembly* were substituted for the word Church. This, we are persuaded, would be impossible.

Though the meaning of the word *Church* is in Scripture always the same, let it be observed that its applications are various. It is applied, at the pleasure of the writer, to any society of Christians, however great, or however small. Examples of this fact will not fail to suggest themselves to all who are familiar with the Word of God. We give a few passages as specimens:

Colossians 4:15: "Salute the brethren which are in Laodicea, and Nymphas, and the Church which is in his house." There the term is applied to a *society of Christians* so small as to be able to find accommodation in a private dwelling-house.

Acts 11:22: "Then tidings of these things came unto the ears of the Church which was in Jerusalem." There it means a *society of Christians* residing in the same city, and including, as we know on excellent authority, several thousand persons.

Acts 7:38: "This is he (Moses) that was in the Church in the wilderness with the angel which spake to him in the Mount Sinai, and with our fathers: who received the lively oracles to give unto us." Here the word signifies a *society of Christians* — an assembly of God's people so large as to include a whole nation, consisting at the time of at least two millions in number. The term is also applied to the people of God in the days of David, when residing in Canaan, spread over a great extent of territory, and amounting to many millions. Hebrews 2:12, compared with Psalm 22:22-25.

1 Corinthians 12:28: "And God hath set some in the Church, first, apostles; secondarily, prophets; thirdly, teachers; after that miracles; then gifts of healings, helps, governments, diversities of tongues." Here the term means the *society of Christians* residing on earth; for it was among them, not among the saints in glory, that God raised up men endowed with apostolic and prophetical gifts.

Ephesians 5:25: "Husbands, love your wives, even as Christ also loved the Church, and gave Himself for it." The word is here used to signify the *society of Christians* in the largest sense — all for whom Christ died — the whole family of God — all saints in heaven and all believers on earth, viewed as one great company.

Let it be observed, however, that, amid all this variety of application, the word Church never alters its sense. Its meaning in every occurrence is the same. However applied, it never ceases to signify a *society of Christians;* but whether the society that the inspired writer has in view is great or small, general or particular, is to be learned, not from the term, but from the circumstances in which the term is used. In every instance it is from the context, never from the word itself, that we are to gather whether the society of Christians, intended by the writer, is to be understood of the collective company of God's people in heaven and earth, or only of those on the earth, in a nation, in a city, or in a private house. The practice — into which the best expositors of Scripture are occasionally betrayed — of taking up some idea conveyed by the context only, and regarding that idea as entering into the meaning of some particular word, has been shown by a late eminent critic to be the origin of those numerous significations — perplexing by their very multitude — appended almost to every word in our classical dictionaries, and the prolific source of errors in the interpretation of the Word of God. This is obviously what has led many to suppose that the word Church has two meanings — signifying something different when referring to the universal body of believers, from what it does when denoting the body of believers connected with a particular locality. The truth is, that the word Church has only one meaning, but it has a variety of applications. The term of itself never conveys any idea but a society of Christians; it is the context that invariably determines its general or particular application: It is manifestly inaccurate, therefore, to maintain that an idea, invariably conveyed by the context, enters into the meaning of the term; when, as all must admit, the term, apart from the context, does not suggest either a limited or universal application.

Had we occasion to speak of the several Christian congregations of a province or nation in their separate capacity, it would be quite in accordance with the Scriptural idiom to designate them the *Churches* of that region. None can forget how frequently the apostle speaks of the Churches of Syria and Achaia, Galatia and Asia. So, if we required to speak of the individual congregations of Christians in Ireland — the separate Christian societies scattered over the country — we might denominate them the Churches of Ireland, there being nothing in existing ecclesiastical usages to make such language either unintelligible or liable to be misunderstood. But it deserves to be noticed that, when we use such phrases as the "Established Church of Scotland", the "Episcopal Church of America", or the "Presbyterian Church of Ireland", there is no departure whatever from the Scriptural sense of the word. The meaning of the word in Scripture, as we have seen, invariably is a society of Christians, and this is precisely its meaning in any of the above phrases; the context, at the same time limiting the Christians in question to those professing certain principles, and belonging to a particular country. When we employ, for instance, such a designation as the *Presbyterian Church of Ireland,* the word Church is used precisely in the Scriptural sense to denote a society of Christians, which we learn from the context professes Presbyterian principles and resides in Ireland.

The propriety of applying the term to signify the Christian people of a country, does not arise from the fact that they are ever assembled in one congregation, either personally or by representatives, but from the fact that the mind contemplates them as a collective body. All saints in heaven and believers on earth are styled the *Church,* not because they are assembled either literally or figuratively, but because, in the view of the mind, they are regarded as a great society, separated from the world, and united by common principles into one great brotherhood. And so the Christians of any denomination, though composing a multitude of congregations, may, in their aggregate capacity, be properly styled a Church, not because they are either figuratively or literally assembled, but because, in the view of the mind, they are regarded as a collective body, distinguished from others, and united among themselves, by the profession of a common creed.

It was once doubted whether the Scriptures contain an example of the word Church being applied to the Christians of a *country*. The science of Biblical Criticism has now set that question at rest in all time coming. The true reading of Acts 9:31, is, "Then had the *Church* rest throughout all Judea, and Galilee, and Samaria; and walking in the fear of the Lord, and in the comfort of the Holy Ghost, *was* multiplied." No man, with the slightest pretensions to scholarship, can now hesitate about receiving this as the original form of the text, when it is known that the lately discovered MS. — the *Codex Sinaiticus* — is in its favour, no less than A B C; these four being at once the most ancient and valuable manuscripts of the New Testament now extant.* Not to speak of the evidence derivable from versions and Fathers, the united voice of these four MSS. is enough to settle the correct form of any text; their testimony as to the original reading of Acts 9:31 none can question; and to that passage we confidently point as a clear instance of the word *Church* being applied to the Christians of a country, viewed as one collective society, though in reality divided into many separate congregations.

Some writers, indeed, give a different account of the matter. They tell us that the universal community of Christians in heaven and on earth is called in Scripture the *Church,* not because they are viewed as one great brotherhood, united by common principles, but because they "are at all times truly and properly assembled in Jesus". It is a mere fancy to suppose that the mind ever takes such a fact into account, when employing the term in its universal application; but, if so, it does not alter the case. The Christians of a particular district, or of a province, or of a nation, may be properly designated a Church for the same reasons; because they also "are at all times truly and properly assembled in Jesus". There is no sense in which all the Christians on earth and in heaven are "assembled in Jesus", that the Christians of any particular country are not thus assembled. If the whole is assembled, so also are the parts. Take the matter either way, the Christians of a district, or a province, or a kingdom, holding certain principles in common, if viewed as a collective community, are a Church, exactly in the sense of the Scriptures. They are a *Society of Christians.*

[* There is solid evidence for believing that these manuscripts are not at all as accurate as the author assumes. See, for example, Pickering, *The Identity of the New Testament Text,* Thomas Nelson Publishers, revised edition 1980.]

GOVERNMENT OF THE CHURCH

THE CHRISTIAN SOCIETY on earth, or, as it is usually called, the Church, is represented in the Scriptures as a *kingdom.* It was of His Church that the Lord Jesus spake, when He said to Pilate, "My kingdom is not of this world" (John 18:36). The fact of its being a kingdom necessarily implies at least three things — first, a *king* or governor; secondly, *subjects;* thirdly, *laws.* In the Church or kingdom of God, the king is *Christ;* the subjects are *believers;* the laws are the *Scriptures* of truth.

Every king has officers under him, who are charged with the execution of his laws, and who have authority from the crown to do justice and judgment. Judges and magistrates are the office-bearers of a kingdom, deriving their power from the monarch under whom they serve, and putting the laws in force among all ranks and classes of the people. Hence a very palpable division of a kingdom is into *rulers* and *ruled* — those whose duty is to administer the law, and those who are bound to obey it.

The same distinction holds in the kingdom of Christ. It also consists of rulers and ruled — the office-bearers entrusted with the dispensation of the laws, and the people who are commanded to yield them submission. This is very plain, from Hebrews 13:17: "Obey them that have the rule over you, and submit yourselves: for they watch for your souls, as they that must give account." It is clear from this passage that there are some in the Church whose duty is to rule; they are the office-bearers of the Church. It is no less clear that there are others in the Church, whose duty is to obey; they are the private members — the subjects of the kingdom — the people.

But in every society where it is the acknowledged duty of some parties to exercise authority, and of others to practise submission, there must be what is called *government;* for in such authority exercised on the one hand, and in such submission rendered on the other, the essence of all government consists. Even was there no passage in the Scriptures but that last quoted, bearing upon the subject, it is undeniable that government was established in the Apostolic Church. If government existed, some *form* of government must have been adopted; for to say that there was established in the kingdom of Christ government without a form of government is absurd. History tells us of many ecclesiastical and political wonders, but of all the strange things that have been witnessed in the world or in the Church, since the beginning of time, there has never yet appeared government without a form of government. The thing is impossible. Government in itself is an abstraction. The moment it puts forth power, it becomes a reality — it stands before the world as a visible thing — it assumes a form.

That there was government in the Apostolic Church, and that this government existed under a certain form, seems clear to demonstration. To determine with precision what this form was, is a matter of great consequence; for it must be evident to all that a plan of Church government, instituted by the apostles of the Lord, acting under the guidance of the Holy Spirit, must carry with it a degree of lawfulness and authority that no human system, though in itself a masterpiece of wisdom — made venerable by age, or recommended by expediency — ever can exhibit; and that every existing form of Church government is deserving of respect only so far as it conforms in its principles to that Divine original. But there are obvious reasons that make it a matter of some difficulty to ascertain with accuracy the system of ecclesiastical polity that was established in the New Testament Church.

(1) The apostles, writing to Christians who were themselves members of the Apostolic Church, and of course well acquainted with its organisation, did not judge it necessary to enter into detailed descriptions of the Christian society. To do so would have been unnatural. They do occasionally state facts bearing on Church government, and hint indirectly at prevailing practices. These hints and facts were sufficiently suggestive and intelligible to the persons originally addressed, but by us, who live in a distant age, in a foreign country, and among associations widely different, they are not so easily understood.

(2) They do not even arrange such facts as bear upon the question in systematic order. If man had had the making of the Bible, it would have been a very different book; but as that circumstance was not left to our option, we must take it as we find it. On examination, we see that it teaches nothing in scientific order. Even morality and doctrine are not there arranged in regular system, but are conveyed in detached portions, and our industry is stimulated by having to gather the scattered fragments, to compare them with each other, and to work them up into order for ourselves. So ecclesiastical polity is not taught in Scripture methodically; but away over the wide field of revelation, facts and hints and circumstances lie scattered, which we are to search for, and examine, and combine, and classify. Now, all do not agree in the arrangement of these facts, nor in the inferences that legitimately flow from them, nor in the mode of constructing a system from the detached material.

These things make it difficult to ascertain with accuracy, and still more so with unanimity, the form of Church government that existed in apostolic days. But difficult as it seems, it is proved quite possible, by a thorough and unprejudiced examination of the Scriptures, to discover the main principles that entered into the constitution of the primitive Church. We say the *main principles* — more than these we need not expect to find. The Word of God, except in some rare instances, never enters into details — it states principles. This is a very noticeable peculiarity of the Divine legislation, that deserves a passing remark.

In every civilised country, it may be observed how those entrusted with the duty of government aim to provide a law for every specific case. The human legislator descends to details. The result of this in our own country is, that the common and statute laws of England are so bulky that the books in which they are written would make of themselves a magnificent library; Parliament meets every year for the express purpose of constructing new, and amending old laws, to suit the ever varying circumstances of the country and the times; and notwithstanding all, cases occur daily in the public courts, wherein the most accomplished jurists have to acknowledge that the existing laws determine nothing. But observe how the Divine law proceeds on a method quite different. It rarely enters into specific details, but lays down general principles, any one of which is quite sufficient to decide a whole multitude of cases. Instead, for instance, of attempting to prescribe every form of good that it is right for a man to perform to his neighbour, it lays down a principle quite sufficient to meet every case — Thou shalt love thy neighbour as thyself. Instead of enumerating the different ways by which children are to discharge the duties that they owe their parents, Scripture enacts this general law, holding good in every case — Honour thy father and thy mother. Declining to specify every semblance of sin that it were well for Christians to avoid, the statutes of the Lord direct us to Abstain from all appearance of evil. Human legislation enters into minute details, but Divine legislation enacts general principles. The result is that, while there is perhaps more room left for difference of opinion in the interpretation and application of the enactments of a code of law constructed on the latter system, yet this disadvantage is more than counterbalanced by the fact, that the laws of God are in themselves perfect; that they do not change with the ever varying circumstances of countries and of times; that they meet every case which can possibly occur; and that they are compressed into a reasonable size, being all written in a book so small that it can be lifted in the hand, or carried in the pocket. Now, the Scripture teaches us Church government, as it teaches morality. It does not furnish minute details, but it supplies *the great leading principles* that entered into the polity of the Apostolic Church. What these main principles were, it is now our purpose to ascertain.*

It is the common practice of writers, in discussing the important subject of ecclesiastical government, to select some one of our modern Churches which happens to be a favourite, delineate its characteristic features, and then proceed to show that they are a reflection of the pattern presented in the Word of God. That this plan has some recommendations, we can readily believe, but it is no less obvious that it is liable to grave objections. It seems to assume at the commencement the conclusion to which the reasoner can only hope to conduct

---

* This paragraph was suggested by reading Dr. Paley's sermon on Romans 14:7.

us after a sound process of logic. It somehow produces the fatal impression, that the writer has determined in the first place that his view of the subject is right, and then goes to Scripture to search for proof of it. The author may be the most impartial and truth-loving of men, but his very plan betrays a preference for some particular system, and thus, at the outset, awakes the prejudices of many readers. Besides, it affords opportunities, for viewing passages of Scripture apart from their connection, and tempts writers to quote in their favourite texts, the sound of which only is upon their side. For these reasons we do not choose to adopt this method on the present occasion.

The plan of procedure we propose is more unusual, though, we trust, not less satisfactory. We will examine the Holy Scriptures with a view of ascertaining from them the various facts that bear on the government of the Apostolic Church. We will produce the passages, contemplate them in their immediate connection, unfold their meaning, and try if, by their aid, we can arrive at *great principles*. We will then turn to our modern Churches, view the different forms of ecclesiastical polity that exist in the world at present, and see which of them it is that embodies all or most of these principles. When this is done, we shall have found the denomination that, in point of government, is best entitled to be regarded as the *Apostolic Church*.

This process of reasoning is so very clear and simple that there is no room for practising deception either on ourselves or our readers. The very humblest intellect may follow our logic to the close. There are but two steps till we arrive at the conclusion. *First,* we are to ascertain from the unerring Word of God what were the main principles in the government of the Churches founded by the apostles of the Lord; and, *secondly,* we are to ascertain in which of our modern Churches these main principles are most fully acknowledged and carried out. We will then apply to the settlement of the matter an axiom, radiant in the light of its own self-evidence. That axiom is, *the modern Church which embodies in its government most apostolic principles, comes nearest in its government to the Apostolic Church.*

CHAPTER TWO

Apostolic Principles

FROM A CAREFUL EXAMINATION of the Scripture, we find at least four different kinds of office-bearers in the Apostolic Church: (1) Apostles; (2) Evangelists; (3) Bishops (also called pastors and teachers); (4) Deacons. Each one of these had a right to exercise all the offices inferior to his own; but one filling an inferior, had no right to discharge the duties of a superior office. Thus, the apostolic office included all the others; and a bishop or elder had the right to act as a deacon, so long as his doing so did not impede the due discharge of duties peculiarly his own. A deacon, on the other hand, had no right to exercise the office of a bishop; nor had a bishop any authority to take on him the duties of an apostle. Each superior office included all below it.

Two of these offices — those of apostle and evangelist — were temporary, necessary at the first establishment of Christianity, but not necessary to be perpetuated. The *apostles* were witnesses of the resurrection of the Lord Jesus, endowed with the power of working miracles and of conferring the Holy Ghost by the laying on of their hands, the infallible expounders of the Divine will, and the founders of the Christian Church; and, having served the purpose for which they were sent, they disappeared out of the world, and, as apostles, have left no successors. *Evangelists* were missionaries — men who travelled from place to place preaching the Gospel, and who acted as the assistants and delegates of the apostles in organising Churches. Of these, Philip and Timothy and Titus were the most eminent examples. It deserves to be remarked, with regard to these temporary, or, as they are usually called, extraordinary office-bearers, that their sphere of duty was not limited to a congregation, but extended to the Church at large. They were members of any Christian Society, within whose bounds they resided for a time, but their mission was to the world, and their authority extended to the Church universal.

The offices of *bishop* and *deacon* were, on the other hand, designed to be perpetual in the Church. The bishops, or, as they are more usually called, elders*, and pastors, and teachers, were office-bearers, whose duty it was to instruct and govern the Church. The deacons had charge of temporal concerns, and were entrusted with the special duty of ministering to the necessities of the poor. The Church can never cease to have need of these two offices, so long as its members have spiritual and temporal wants to be supplied. But it is to be observed, with regard to the bishops and deacons, that they were mainly cong-regational officers. The sphere of their duty was not so general as that of the apostles, prophets, and evangelists, but lay for the most part within the bounds of that particular Church or district for which they were appointed to act.

Dr. Campbell thus expounds the special necessity that existed in the primitive Church, both for the temporary and perpetual office-bearers: "To take a similitude from temporal things: It is one thing to conquer a kingdom and become master of it, and another thing to govern it when conquered, so as to retain the possession which has been acquired. The same agents and the same expedients are not properly adapted to both. For the first of these purposes, there was a set of extraordinary ministers or officers in the Church, who, like the military forces intended for conquest, could not be fixed to a particular spot whilst there remained any provinces to conquer. Their charge was, in a manner, universal, and their functions ambulatory. For the second, there was a set of ordinary ministers or pastors, corresponding to civil governors, to whom it was necessary to allot distinct charges or precincts, to which their services were chiefly to be confined, in order to instruct the people, to preside in the public worship and religious ordinances, and to give them the necessary assistance for the regulation of their conduct. Without this second arrangement, the acquisi-tions made could not have been long retained. There must have ensued an universal relapse into idolatry and infidelity. This distinction of ministers into extraordinary and ordinary, has been admitted by controvertists on both sides, and therefore cannot justly be considered as introduced (which sometimes happens to distinctions) to serve an hypothesis."† With these preliminary observations, we proceed in search of —

---

* This is assumed for the present: it will be proved afterwards.

† Lectures on Ecclesiastical History. Lecture 4, 3rd edition. London, 1824.

THE FIRST PRINCIPLE

ALL OFFICES in the Christian Church take origin from the Lord Jesus. Himself is the Author and embodiment of them all; He is the Apostle of our profession; He is an Evangelist, preaching peace to them that are afar off, and to them that are nigh; He is the great Pastor or Shepherd of the sheep — the Bishop of souls; and He is the Deacon or servant who came not to be ministered to, but to minister. All offices in the Church are embodied in the person of Christ.

The apostles were the only office-bearers chosen during the lifetime of the Lord. They held their appointments immediately from Himself. They were called to the work of the ministry by His voice, and they received their commission at His hands. Simon and Andrew were casting their nets into the Lake of Galilee, as Jesus walked upon the beach, but at His call they left their nets to follow Him through the world. The sons of Zebedee heard His voice, and forthwith they forgot both father and mother in their ambition to become fishers of men. When Christ said, Follow me, Levi forsook the receipt of custom, and was a publican no more. The personal call of the Lord Jesus was then, and is still, the first and best of all authority to hold office in the Church of God. Let a man only satisfy us that he holds his appointment directly from the Lord, as the apostles did, and we require no more to induce us to submit to him.

But after the Lord has ascended to heaven, the personal call, except in case of Paul, who was one born out of due time, was not the passport of any man either to the ministry or apostleship. Men were no more put into office by the living voice of the Lord Jesus. The departure of the Master, and the vacancy left in the list of apostles by the death of Judas, gave opportunity for bringing into operation a new principle. The first chapter of the Acts of the Apostles brings the whole case before us. Let us specially examine the passage — Acts 1:13-26 — that we may have full possession of the facts. It appears that, in the interval between the Ascension and the Day of Pentecost, the disciples met for prayer and supplication in an upper room of the city of Jerusalem. The mother and brethren of Jesus were present, as were also the eleven apostles. Taken together, they numbered one hundred and twenty in all. Peter rose and addressed the company. He reminded them of the vacancy in the apostleship. Judas, who betrayed the Master, was dead, and the office that he forfeited by his transgression must be conferred upon another. He states the necessary qualifications of him who was to be the successor of Judas. He must be one who had intercourse with the eleven from the commencement of Christ's ministry to the close. He states the duties of the new apostle; he was to be with the others a witness of Christ's resurrection. Such was the case that Peter put before the men and brethren, met together in that upper room of Jerusalem. We then read in verse 23, *"They appointed two,* Joseph called Barsabas, who was surnamed Justus, and Matthias."* In consequence of this double choice, it became necessary to decide which should be regarded as the true apostle; which, after prayer, was done by casting lots. But let it be particularly observed that, while Peter explained the necessary qualifications, and the peculiar duties of the office, the appointment of the person did not rest with Peter, but with the men and brethren to whom the address of Peter was directed. Farther, it is not to be forgotten that the office to which Matthias succeeded is, in the 20th verse, termed a *bishoprick,* and how it is said in the 25th verse, he had "to take part of this *ministry* and apostleship". The men and brethren, at the instigation of Peter, exercised the right of appointing a man to a bishopric — that is, to the office of a bishop, and to take part in the ministry. In the Apostolic Church, the people appointed Matthias to be a minister — a bishop — an apostle. The case recorded in Acts 14:23, is to the same effect, though, from a mistranslation, the force of it is lost upon the English reader. The Authorised Version represents the two apostles, Barnabas and Paul, as *ordaining* elders in every church; whereas the true meaning of the word in the original is "to elect by a show of hands" — a fact now admitted by the best expositors.* We must not allow a faulty translation to rob us of the testimony of Scripture to an important fact — namely, that the elders of the New Testament Church were appointed to office by the popular vote.

The sixth chapter of Acts comes next under consideration. At the period to which the narrative there recorded refers, the disciples at Jerusalem had grown numerous. The Grecians began to complain against the Hebrews, how that their widows were neglected in the daily ministrations. Hitherto the twelve had attended to the wants of the poor; but their hands were at the same time full of other work, and, among such a multitude, it is not surprising that some were neglected, nor is it very wonderful, considering what human nature is, that some were found to murmur, even when apostles managed the business. What was now to be done? A division of offices was clearly a necessity. But were the apostles to take it on themselves to select persons on whom should devolve the duty of attending to the temporal wants of the community? Had they done so, few would dispute their right, or venture to charge inspired men with the exercise of a despotic or unwarranted authority. But, instead of this, they adopted a course of procedure unaccountable to us on any other principle, than that they purposely managed the matter in such a way as would guide the Church in the appointment of office-bearers when themselves would be removed, and thus form a precedent for future ages. The apostles summoned the multitude

---

* See Dean Alford on the passage.

together and explained the case. They said their appropriate business as ministers was with the Word of God. They said it was unreasonable for them to have to neglect the spiritual province, in order to attend to temporal concerns; and they called upon the brethren to look out among themselves for seven men, of good character, gifted with wisdom and the Spirit of God, who might be appointed to take charge of this secular business, and who would leave the apostles free to attend to duties peculiarly their own — namely, prayer and the ministry of the Word. "And the saying pleased the whole multitude; and *they chose* Stephen, a man full of faith and of the Holy Ghost, and Philip, and Prochorus, and Nicanor, and Timon, and Parmenas, and Nicolas, a proselyte of Antioch; whom they set before the apostles; and when they had prayed, they laid their hands on them" (Acts 6:5-6). The seven men whom the multitude chose on this occasion were the first *deacons*. Though not expressly called so in the Scriptures, yet they are admitted to have been such, by almost universal consent. The lowest office-bearers, therefore, in the Apostolic Church, were chosen by the people.

Here, then, are three clear facts, fully sufficient to be the basis of a principle. The first chapter of Acts supplies us with an instance of the assembled men and brethren appointing to office one who was both an apostle and a minister. The fourteenth chapter shows that the elders of the congregation were chosen by popular suffrage. The sixth chapter furnishes an example of the whole multitude of the disciples choosing seven men to be deacons. On these three facts, clear and irresistible, we found the principle of *Popular Election*. The conclusion that follows from this evidence, we find it absolutely impossible to evade, namely — that in the Apostolic Church the *office-bearers were chosen by the people*.

THE SECOND PRINCIPLE

THERE IS A CLASS of office-bearers very frequently mentioned as existing in the early Church, and to which, as yet, we have only made a slight allusion. We mean the *elder,* or *presbyter,* as he is frequently called. This church officer is often mentioned in the Acts and Epistles; but an attentive reader will not fail to remark that no passage of Scripture ever speaks of him as holding an office distinct from the *bishop*. The same verse never speaks of bishops and elders. When Paul, for example, writes to the Philippian Church (1:1), he mentions the bishops and deacons, but says nothing of elders. When James directs the sick to call for the elders of the Church (5:14), he says nothing of bishops. If the offices of bishop and elder were quite distinct — if a bishop were an office-bearer bearing rule over a number of elders, it does seem strange that no passage of Scripture speaks at the same time of bishops and elders. There is one supposition, and only one, that would furnish a satisfactory reason for this fact. If the two terms be only different names for the same office, then to speak of *bishops* and *elders* would be a violation of the laws of language — it would be tautology — it would be the same thing as to speak of presbyters and elders, or of bishops *and* bishops. To suppose that the two offices were identical accounts sufficiently for the significant fact that they are never mentioned together in the same passage of the Word of God; for it is plain that one of the terms being adequate to indicate the office-bearer intended, there was no need to introduce the other at the same time.

Still there must be something stronger than a presumption to warrant us in saying that the two terms were only different names for the same person. However improbable it may appear, it is still possible that these two, bishop and elder, were distinct office-bearers even though the same passage never speaks of them together. This obliges us to consult the Scriptures further on this question.

The first passage that comes before us is Titus 1:5-7: "For this cause left I thee in Crete, that thou shouldest set in order the things that are wanting, and ordain elders in every city, as I had appointed thee: if any be blameless, the husband of one wife, having faithful children, not accused of riot or unruly. For a bishop must be blameless, as the steward of God; not self-willed, not soon angry, not given to wine, no striker, not given to filthy lucre." This passage strongly confirms the truth of the supposition already made, that the two offices were identical. It appears that Paul left Titus behind him in Crete to ordain elders in every city. To guide him in the discharge of this duty, the apostle proceeds to state the qualifications of an elder. No private member of the Church was eligible to that office except he was a man of blameless life, the husband of one wife, and had obedient children; "for," says he, "a bishop must be blameless, as the steward of God". Dr. King well observes on this passage, "that the term *elder,* used at the commencement, is exchanged for the term *bishop* in the conclusion, while the same office-bearer is spoken of. An *elder* must have such and such qualifications. Why? Because a *bishop* must be blameless, as the steward of God. Does not this identify the elder and the bishop? If not, identification is impossible. Were it said, the Lord Mayor of London must devote himself to his duties, for the chief magistrate of such a city has great responsibilities, would not the language bear, that the Lord Mayor and the chief magistrate were the same office-bearers? Otherwise, the representation would be absurd; for why should the mayor devote himself to his duties because some other person had great responsibilities? Yet the mayor and chief magistrate are not more identified in this comparison than are the elder and bishop in Paul's instructions to

Titus."* It must be evident to every unprejudiced man that the apostle would never state as a reason for ordaining none but men of good moral character to the office of the *eldership,* that a *bishop* must be blameless, if he did not understand that elder and bishop were only different designations for the same office. On any other supposition, the language of the apostle would be without coherence and without sense.

Again, we turn to 2 John 1, and we find how the apostle John styles himself an *elder* — "The elder unto the elect lady and her children, whom I love in the truth." Next comes up 1 Peter 5:1, and we find there that the apostle Peter calls himself an *elder* — "The elders which are among you I exhort, who am also an elder, and a witness of the sufferings of Christ." That John and Peter were both bishops all admit; but these passages show that they were elders also. This, however, brings us but a step to the conclusion. It may be true that every general is an officer, but it does not follow from this that every officer is a general. A bishop may, like John and Peter, be an elder, but it does not necessarily follow that an elder is a bishop. This may be true, but we require more proof before we can reach such a conclusion. This we have as fully as can be desired in Acts 20:17-28. We read there how Paul sent for the elders of the Church at Ephesus to meet him at Miletus. He spoke of his ministry in their city, the great theme of his preaching being repentance towards God, and faith towards the Lord Jesus Christ. He foretold the afflictions awaiting him at Jerusalem and elsewhere, and he saddened their hearts by saying to them that they would see his face no more. And he warned them to take heed to themselves and to the flock over which the Holy Ghost had made them *overseers* — that is, *bishops,* as the word is elsewhere rendered. Every reader acquainted with the original is aware that the word translated *overseers,* in Acts 20:28, is the very same as that translated *bishops* in Philippians 1:1, so that we have here the evidence of inspiration, that the elders of Ephesus were bishops by appointment of the Holy Ghost. This makes the chain of reasoning strong and conclusive. Bishops, as we have seen, were elders, and elders, as we now see, were bishops. This conducts us to a principle — namely, that, *in the Apostolic Church, the offices of bishop and elder were identical.* An elder was not inferior to a bishop, nor was a bishop superior to an elder. It was the same office-bearer who was known by these different names.

We are not disposed to attach much value to the opinion of such a man as Edward Gibbon, on any question of doctrine or morality, but that distinguished historian was competent to grapple with a matter of fact, and may be heard as one who, from being unprejudiced in favour of any religious system whatever,

---

* King, *Exposition and Defence of the Presbyterian Form of Church Government,* pages 176-7. Edinburgh, 1853.

was in a position to judge impartially in a case of this kind. Speaking of the government and administration of the Church prior to the Council of Nice he says, "The public functions of religion were solely entrusted to the established ministers of the Church, bishops and the presbyters; *two appellations which, in their first origin, appear to have distinguished the same office, and the same order of persons.* The name of *presbyter* was expressive of their age, or rather of their gravity and wisdom. The title of *bishop* denoted their inspection over the faith and manners of the Christians who were committed to their pastoral care."*

THE THIRD PRINCIPLE

LET IT NOT BE FORGOTTEN that we have now ascertained that presbyter and bishop were, in *their first origin,* only different names for the same ecclesiastical office-bearer. Enough has been found in the Scriptures to satisfy us that bishops were elders, and that elders were bishops, in the Apostolic Church. We are warranted, therefore, to regard this fact as fully substantiated, while we proceed to the discovery of a third principle.

The fourteenth chapter of Acts describes a missionary journey of Paul and Barnabas. There was an attempt made to stone them at Iconium, but they fled to Lystra and Derbe. When Paul made a cripple at Lycaonia leap and walk, the priest of Jupiter brought oxen and garlands to the gates, and it was with some difficulty the people in their pagan ignorance were restrained from paying divine honours to the two preachers. But so fickle are the sentiments of the multitude that, shortly afterwards, the great apostle was stoned nearly to death at the very place where he had been almost worshipped as a god. Barely escaping with his life, Paul and his companion revisited Derbe, and Lystra, and Iconium, and Antioch, preaching the Gospel, confirming the souls of the disciples, and exhorting them to continue in the faith. And the sacred historian, in the narrative of this evangelistic tour, informs us of this important fact, that *they appointed elders in every Church.* His words are — "And when they had chosen for them, by suffrage, elders in every Church, and had prayed with fasting, they commended them to the Lord, on whom they believed" (Acts 14:23). We have seen already that a Church in Scripture signifies any assembly of Christians, however great or small. It was the primitive practice to call the believers residing in any town, however large, or in any village, however small, the Church of that place. Many of these societies, collected from among the heathen by these

---

* *History of the Decline and Fall of the Roman Empire,* chapter 15.

pioneers of Christianity, organised in the face of difficulty, and thinned by intimidation, must have been weak in point of numbers. Still, the two apostles were not satisfied with appointing one elder or bishop in each society, however small in numbers; but as we are taught by the Holy Spirit, they appointed *elders in every Church*. If, then, the evangelist Luke, speaking as he was moved by the Holy Ghost, is a true witness, there were more elders than one in each congregation of the Apostolic Church. How many, whether two, three, or more, we are not informed, but that in each Church there was a plurality of elders is clear.

We proceed once more to the twentieth chapter of Acts. Here Paul is represented as travelling from Greece on his way to Jerusalem. Having stopped a week at Troas, he went upon his onward way, sometimes by sea and sometimes by land, striving to reach the Jewish capital before Pentecost. Having touched at Miletus, a seaport of Ionia, thirty-six miles south of Ephesus, he sent a message to that city for the elders of the Church. The words of inspiration are — "And from Miletus he sent to Ephesus, and called the elders of the Church" (Acts 20:17). From this, it appears the Church of Ephesus had not only one elder, but more, and we have already seen that, in verse 28, its elders are called bishops. Unless language mean nothing, and the statements of Scripture be as unintelligible as the leaves of the Sybil, there was *a plurality of elders or bishops* in the Church at Ephesus.

Still farther. Philippi was a city on the confines of ancient Thrace. To the classic reader it is known as the place where Augustus and Antony wrested from Brutus and Cassius, in a pitched battle, the empire of the world; to the Christian it is remarkable as being the first spot in Europe where the banner of the Cross was unfurled, and sinners listened to the Gospel of Jesus. There the heart of the seller of purple was opened to attend to the things that were spoken of Paul. It was there that, for casting the spirit of divination out of a soothsayer, Paul and Silas were beaten by the magistrates, and had their feet made fast in the stocks. It was there at the dead hour of the night, when the foundations of the prison shook, and every door in the jail flew open, and every man's chains fell from his arms, that the keeper of the prison asked two of his prisoners the most important question that was ever put by a sinner to a minister of God — "Sirs, what must I do to be saved?" In this town of Philippi a Church was organised, though in face of determined opposition; and, some ten or twelve years after Paul's first visit, he thought it right to address to this Church a letter. This letter has been preserved. It finds a place in the Word of God. It is that known to us as the Epistle to the Philippians. One has some curiosity to read what an apostle thought it good to write to a Church, at the head of whose roll of members stood the names of Lydia and the Jailer. As might be expected, it is full to the brim of precious and consoling truths; but, what is more to our purpose at present, we find these words in the first verse of the first chapter: "Paul and Timotheus, the servants of Jesus Christ, to all the saints in Christ Jesus which are at Philippi, with *the bishops* and deacons.'' Philippi was, no doubt, a considerable town; but, in point of population and importance, it was no more to such a city as Dublin or Liverpool than a parish is to a diocese. Yet, in modern times, one bishop is thought sufficient even for London, where professing Christians are numbered by millions, whereas a single Christian congregation gathered out of a heathen population, possessing ecclesiastical existence only for ten or twelve years, exposed to contumely and suffering for Christ's sake, and located in a contemptible town on the outskirts of Macedonia, had a *plurality of bishops*. Paul, in writing to that Church, addresses his epistle to the *bishops* and deacons.

Let the candid reader glance again at the ground over which we have passed. He sees that Paul, in writing his epistle to the Church at Philippi, addressed it to the *bishops*. He sees there were *elders* in the Church at Ephesus when Paul sent for them to Miletus. He finds it stated that Barnabas and Paul ordained *elders in every Church*. How is it possible for him to resist the conclusion that, in apostolic days, there was in each congregation a plurality of elders, or what we have seen amounts to the same thing, a plurality of bishops? This leads us to the third principle of apostolic government — that *in each Church there was a plurality of elders.*

THE FOURTH PRINCIPLE

ORDINATION is the solemn designation of a person to ecclesiastical office with the laying on of hands. Every permanent office-bearer in the Church, whether bishop or deacon, was set apart solemnly to his office by the act of ordination. In its outward form it consisted of three things — fasting, prayer and imposition of hands. The imposition of hands was used when spiritual gifts were conferred (Acts 8:17; 19:6); and it was also practised when the sick were miraculously healed (Mark 16:18; Acts 9:17; 28:8). But, distinct from all such cases, the laying on of hands was used at the ordination of Church office-bearers, and when no extraordinary or miraculous gift was bestowed (Acts 6:6; 13:1-3; and 1 Timothy 4:14; 5:22). The withdrawment of miraculous powers cannot therefore be any valid reason why, at ordinations, the practice should be set aside; the imposition of hands in such cases never was the medium of imparting the Holy Ghost, but only the form of investing with ecclesiastical office.

The great question regarding ordination is, whether it is the act of one individual or more, of one elder or many elders, of a bishop or a presbytery? That the Lord Jesus may give a special call to any labourer, and send him to work in His vineyard, none disputes. There can be very little doubt also that, if an inspired apostle were still upon the earth, he would have the right to ordain alone, if he thought it right to do so. Nay, if some modern evangelist could show, as Titus could, that an apostle had left him behind for this special purpose, he, too, in virtue of the right conferred upon him by a higher power, would have the privilege of ordaining (Titus 1:5). Any one, therefore, claiming the right of doing all that an evangelist did, would require to show that, if not an apostle, he possesses, like Titus, the authority delegated to him by an apostle. But here every ruler in every Church must fail. It remains, therefore, that we examine the Scriptures to discover who it was that, in the absence of apostles, or those delegated by apostles, had the privilege of solemnly setting apart others to ecclesiastical office, and especially to ascertain if this power was lodged in one individual or in more.

First, we turn to 1 Timothy 4:14. We have there the ordination of Timothy. The apostle exhorts his son in the faith to employ to good purpose the gift of the ministry that had been conferred upon him. He intimates that this gift had been given by prophecy — that is, in consequence of certain intimations of the prophets, who were numerous in that age of spiritual gifts, marking him out as one who would be an eminent minister. He adds that the gift was conferred *with the laying on of the hands of the presbytery* — that is, by the presbyters or elders in their collective capacity. The words of the apostle are — "Neglect not the gift that is in thee, which was given thee by prophecy, *with the laying on of the hands of the presbytery.*" These words are decisive as to the parties with whom the power of ordination is lodged.

Again, we turn to Acts 13:1-3. It appears that, in the Church of Antioch, there were certain prophets and teachers whose names are there recorded. They ministered to the Lord and fasted; and, while thus employed, it was intimated to them by the Holy Ghost that they should separate Barnabas and Saul for missionary work among the Gentiles. Both had been preachers of the Gospel previously; but now they were to enter on a new sphere, and engage in a new department of the work. It was right, therefore, that the prophets and teachers should solemnly set apart the two brethren to the missionary work by the act of ordination. We read, accordingly, in verse 3, that "when *they* had fasted and prayed, and *laid their hands on them,* they sent them away". The act of ordination was here evidently not the work of one teacher, but of several. A plurality took part in it.

Another instance of a plurality of Church rulers taking part in this rite is recorded in Acts 6:6. We have there the ordination of the deacons. The Church at Jerusalem chose seven men to attend to the necessities of the poor, "whom they set before the apostles: and when they had prayed, *they laid their hands* on them". This is particularly valuable, as it proves that, when it was convenient or practicable for a plurality of rulers to take part in the act of ordination, the apostles themselves preferred that course.

Glance again at the ground over which we have now passed. It was the practice of an apostle, or one directly appointed by an apostle for this specific purpose, to perform alone the act of ordination. But they did not ordain singly where it was possible for them to associate. Where a plurality could be had conveniently, as in the case of the deacons, it was common for more than one to take part in the ceremony. In the absence of apostles we have seen, in the case of Saul and Barnabas, ordination was the act of certain prophets and teachers; and, in the case of Timothy, it was the act of the presbytery. This conducts us to our fourth principle, namely, that, *in the Apostolic Church, ordination was the act of the presbytery* — of a plurality of elders.

THE FIFTH PRINCIPLE

THE FIFTEENTH CHAPTER of Acts is much too long to be here transcribed. But, before the reader proceeds farther, let him open the Bible and read that chapter carefully from the commencement to the close. If he is really in search of truth, and diposed to receive it in its simplicity, the perusal of that chapter will satisfy him that the following facts are there embodied:

It appears that certain men came down from Judea to Antioch, and taught the Church there that circumcision is necessary to salvation. Paul and Barnabas set themselves to oppose these teachers, but in vain. It was then agreed that certain of the Church of Antioch, including in their number Barnabas and Paul, should go up to Jerusalem and lay the case before the apostles and elders. When they reached Jerusalem — at that time the metropolis of Christianity — the apostles and elders came together to consider the question. At first there was in the assembly considerable difference of opinion. Peter at last rose to speak. He reminded them how God had honoured him in making him the instrument of first preaching the Gospel to the Gentiles, and how it had pleased God, without respect of persons, to bestow the Holy Ghost upon them as well as upon Jewish believers. He argues, therefore, that to make circumcision necessary to salvation — to bind a yoke upon the Gentiles which even the Jews were not able to bear — would be to tempt God; and he closes by enunciating the great truth that Jews and Gentiles, both alike, obtain salvation through the grace of our Lord Jesus Christ. Barnabas and Paul followed, declaring that by them, too, God had wrought among the Gentiles miracles and wonders. James next delivered his opinion. He showed that the truth declared by Peter, namely, that God had taken out of the Gentiles a people for His name, was the subject of ancient prophecy. He quotes from the prophet Amos to show how God had promised to build the tabernacle of David which had fallen into ruins, that the residue of men and the Gentiles called by His name should seek after the Lord. He ends by declaring his judgment to be, that the Gentiles already turned to the Lord should not be troubled with any unnecessary burden, but that they should be directed to abstain from pollutions of idols, and from fornication, and from things strangled, and from blood. The opinion of James was approved by the assembly. The apostles and elders, with the whole Church, agreed to send Judas and Silas down to Antioch, with Barnabas and Paul to announce the result. The decision of the meeting was embodied in letters, which ran in the name of the apostles, elders, and brethren, and were addressed to the Gentile Christians in Antioch, Syria, and Cilicia. The epistle charged those who taught that circumcision was necessary to salvation with troubling the brethren, and subverting their souls; denied that they had authority from the apostles and elders so to teach; mentioned that Judas and Silas were empowered, along with Barnabas and Paul — men who hazarded their lives for the name of the Lord Jesus — to declare verbally the decision of the assembly; and stated that it seemed good to the Holy Ghost and to them to impose upon the Gentile converts no burden except abstinence from meats offered to idols, from blood, from things strangled, and from fornication. Such was the substance of the letter that was carried down to Antioch by the deputies from the assembly at Jerusalem. The multitude gathered to hear it; it was delivered and read, and the people rejoiced for the consolation. Judas and Silas added their exhortations, and the brethren were confirmed in the faith. Shortly afterwards, Paul, having had some difference with Barnabas, chose Silas as his fellow-traveller, and set out on another missionary journey, the object of which was to visit the converts in every city where he had preached the Word of God, and see how they did. Commended by the brethren to the grace of God, Paul and Silas departed from Antioch, and went through Syria and Cilicia confirming the churches. Derbe and Lystra and other cities of Asia Minor were visited on this occasion, and, as they went through the cities, they delivered to them the decrees for to keep which were ordained of the apostles and elders that were at Jerusalem (Acts 16:4).

Every candid man must admit that this is a fair representation of all facts bearing on the subject, as put before us in the fifteenth and sixteenth chapters of the Acts. Let it be remarked that, in the simple narrative, the following facts stand noticeably out:

(1) That Barnabas and Paul had a dispute about circumcision with certain false teachers who came down from Judea;

(2) This dispute was not settled in the Church of Antioch where it originated;

(3) The matter was referred to an external ecclesiastical assembly consisting of the apostles and elders at Jerusalem;

(4) This assembly met publicly to deliberate on the question;

(5) They pronounced a decision;

(6) To this decision the Church of Antioch and the Churches of Syria and Cilicia yielded submission.

These facts are on the face of the narrative, and cannot be denied. That they were permitted to take place, and that a record of them is inserted in the Holy Scriptures, seems strange if these things did not happen for an example to us. Were it enough for the Church of Antioch to be made certain of the mind of God upon the point in dispute, Paul, who was present, could have declared this with infallible accuracy; for he was one who not only spake as he was moved by the Holy Ghost, but who often decided matters equally important by a word from his lips or a stroke of his pen. A single sentence from the very apostle who was then at Antioch is admitted by the Church of God to be decisive on any point of Christian faith or Christian duty; so that, if an infallible decision was the only thing required, one does not see why the matter was ever carried farther. When the case did come up to Jerusalem, had the appeal been to inspiration only, one does not see what business the elders had to meet with the apostles to consider the matter; surely the apostles were competent to declare the mind of God without the aid of uninspired men. If nothing was necessary but for the apostles to pronounce an infallible deliverance, why was there such a thing as disputing in the assembly, or even the semblance of deliberation, or why should one apostle after another state his opinion? We would suppose the deliverance of a single inspired man quite sufficient. If the disputing that occurred in the assembly was only among the elders, the elders must have been very silly to dispute about a matter that inspiration was to settle, and with which they, as uninspired men, could have nothing to do, but to listen to the voice of God; and why did the apostles permit them to dispute, when a word from the infallible expounders of the Divine will could have decided the question? And when the decree went forth, why was it in the name of the apostles and *elders* that were at Jerusalem? There is one way of accounting for this satisfactorily, and only one so far as we can see. These events were permitted to take place, and are recorded for our guidance under all similar circumstances. Should any difference arise, which cannot be settled within the limits of the congregation where it occurs, it is to be referred for settlement to the rulers of the Church in their assembled capacity. If the apostles were alive upon the earth to meet with the elders, and by aid of their inspiration, to guide them to an unerring decision, and were we to refer our differences to such an assembly, this would be literal obedience to the example put before us in the Divine Word. But when, in their personal absence, we refer our differences to the assembly of the elders, and when the elders, guided by the inspired writings of the apostles as contained in the Scriptures, pronounce a deliverance on the question, and when to such deliverance we yield submission in the Lord, this is more than acting up to the spirit, it is acting up to everything but the letter, of apostolic example.

We are thus conducted to this twofold fact that, in the Apostolic Church, there existed the privilege of referring disputed matters to the decision of an assembly of living men, external to the congregation where such dispute originated, and composed of the rulers of the Church; and that this ecclesiastical assembly, in the absence of the apostles, consisting simply of the rulers of the Church, has a right to meet, to deliberate, to decide, and to demand obedience to its decisions in the Lord. This twofold principle we designate *the privilege of appeal to the assembly of elders, and the right of government exercised by them in their associate capacity.*

It would scarcely be necessary to say a word on the presence of the *brethren* in the assembly at Jerusalem, were it not that some parties have made this fact the foundation for special cavil. As they are mentioned separately from the apostles and elders, it seems to us clear that the "brethren" must have been the non-official members of the Church, or, as in modern times they would be called, the laity. That they were present at the meeting; that they concurred in the decision; and that the letter sent down to Antioch was written in their name, as well as in that of the apostles and elders, are, in our opinion, undeniable facts — patent on the face of the narrative. But we have not all the facts of the case before us, except we observe —

(1) That the original reference from Antioch was not to the brethen, but to the apostles and elders (verse 2);

(2) That it is not said that the brethren assembled to deliberate on the question, but that "the apostles and elders came together for to consider of this matter" (verse 6);

(3) That we do not read of any of the brethren speaking on the subject submitted, but that they "kept silence" while others spoke (verse 12);

(4) That the decrees are not said to be ordained of the brethren, but "of the apostles and elders which were at Jerusalem" (Acts 16:4).

The unprejudiced inquirer will observe that the private members of the Church, here designated the "brethren", did not ordain the decrees, nor speak in the meeting, nor assemble to deliberate, nor was it to them that the appeal from Antioch was brought. He will, on the other hand, remark that they were present in the assembly, that they concurred in the finding, and that, as it was important to show that all the Christians of Jerusalem were unanimous on the subject, the letter embodying the decision was written in their name as well as in that of the apostles and elders. From motives of courtesy, and for the purpose of Christian salutation, Silvanus and Timotheus are represented as uniting with Paul, in his First Epistle to the Thessalonians, but this does not imply that Silvanus and Timotheus were inspired men, much less that they were conjoined in the authorship of the letter. And, in the same way, the letter addressed to the Gentiles of Antioch, Syria, and Cilicia, was the letter of the apostles and elders — the name of the brethren being added to show, not that they took part in the composition, but that they concurred in the sentiments. Persons, therefore, who desire to convince us that private Christians in the Apostolic Church were not only present as auditors at assemblies of Church rulers, but also shared in the deliberations, and acted as constituent members of ecclesiastical courts, would require to produce something much more explicit on the subject than the fifteenth chapter of Acts. To us it seems clear that the apostles and elders assembled, deliberated, and decreed; the brethren were present, listened, and concurred. The apostles and elders were, as we would say, members of court; the brethren were only auditors, who gave their assent to the decision of the rulers.

Our fifth principle, therefore, may be summed up in these terms — *the privilege of appeal to the assembly of elders, and the right of government exercised by them in their corporate character.*

THE SIXTH PRINCIPLE

IT IS A DISTINCTIVE FEATURE of the apostolic government that Church rulers did not render spiritual obedience to any temporal potentate, or to any ecclesiastical chief. Paul seldom commences any of his epistles without reminding his readers that he held his apostleship by the will of God, not by the favour of man. Take, as an example, Galatians 1:1: "Paul an apostle (not of men, neither by man, but by Jesus Christ, and God the Father who raised Him from the dead)," etc. In the picture of apostolic times presented in the New Testament, we can detect no instance of the Church acknowledging the spiritual dominion of any earthly monarch, or consenting to surrender a portion of its religious liberty for any temporal advantage whatever. We find no provision made in the Gospel for the supremacy of a Christian, much less of a heathen, king in the things of God. The law of Scripture is express: "Render to Caesar the things that are Caesar's, and to God the things that are God's" (Mark 12:17). In all temporal matters the members of the Apostolic Church regarded it their duty to yield obedience to the civil rulers of the country in which they lived; in all spiritual matters they did homage to a higher power. In temporal matters an apostle bowed to the laws of the land as administered by the magistrate of a village; in spiritual matters he would not bow to Caesar on his throne.

It does not alter the case to say that we look in vain for such an example to the Scriptures, owing to the fact that, in the primitive age, no temporal prince was made a convert to Christianity, and therefore none was in circumstances to dispense ecclesiastical patronage and serve as the depository of spiritual power. But God is not limited by want of instruments. The same grace that subdued Saul of Tarsus, at a time when he was breathing out slaughter against the saints of the Lord, could have converted Pilate, or Agrippa, or Caesar at Rome. Had the example been useful, the necessary means of supplying the example would not have been lacking to God. The very fact that, in apostolic days, God did not take some heathen prince and make a Christian of him, in order that he might fill the office of temporal head of the Church on earth, is in itself an instructive fact — fraught with a moral. And let it be remarked that the Scriptures make no provision for such an occurrence in after times. They contain no principle authorising the prince either to claim or exercise authority in ecclesiastical matters, when in the course of ages a Christian potentate would appear. If there be such a principle it is unknown to us; and it is certainly incumbent on those who approve of such an arrangement, to produce from the Scriptures, if they can, their warrant for maintaining that a Christian king has a right to exercise supremacy over the Church in spiritual matters. Till this is done we must be excused for believing that no temporal prince has a right to act as a lord over the heritage of God.

Nor was supreme spiritual power lodged in the hands of any office-bearer of the Church, however distinguished by his gifts, his sufferings, or his abundant labours. The private members, indeed, had it in command to obey the rulers or elders of the Church; but the elders, on their part, were enjoined not to act as lords over God's heritage, but to be examples to the flock (1 Peter 5:3). Even the apostles did not claim to have dominion over the people's faith, but only to be helpers of their joy (2 Corinthians 1:24). And among these apostles it does not appear that pre-eminence was vested in any. Peter is the only one for whom, in later times, official supremacy is ever claimed; but he never claimed it for himself; he always acted with his fellow apostles as a simple preacher of the cross of Christ; he is never presented in the Scriptures as nominating to ecclesiastical office, or as exercising any peculiar control over the inferior officers in the Church. On one noted occasion, when he exhibited some tergiversation, we are told of another apostle who withstood him to the face, because he was to be blamed (Galatians 2:11). The Scripture, therefore, furnishes no ground whatever for believing that supreme spiritual power is deposited in any ecclesiastical officer any more than in any temporal prince.

The Scriptures are to be our guide on this as well as on all other religious matters. We turn to the following passages, and find where the source of all spiritual power exists:

Ephesians 1:20-23: "Which He (God) wrought in Christ, when He raised Him from the dead, and set Him at His own right hand in the heavenly places, far above all principality, and power, and might, and dominion, and every name that is named, not only in this world, but also in that which is to come, and hath put all things under His feet, and gave *Him to be the head over all things to the Church,* which is His body, the fulness of Him that filleth all in all."

Ephesians 5:23: "For the husband is the head of the wife, even *as Christ is the head of the Church;* and He is the Saviour of the body."

Colossians 1:18: "And He (Christ) *is the head of the body, the Church:* who is the beginning, the firstborn from the dead; that in all things He might have the pre-eminence."

The passages now quoted are taken from the Holy Scriptures — the only rule of Christian faith and practice. We have given them our attentive consideration: and they have led us to the conclusion that *the sole headship of Christ over the Church* was the doctrine of apostolic days. What the head is to the human body Christ is to the Church; and as the body cannot have two heads, so the Church cannot have two heads — neither Christ and the pope, nor Christ and the monarch. To us there seems no middle way in this matter. We must either reject the authority of the Bible, or believe what it teaches — namely, that *Christ is head over all things to the Church.* We choose the latter. The *Headship of Christ* is the sixth principle of government that we find in operation in apostolic days. Let us observe the consequence of this principle; for as Christ is the Head of the Church, the members of the Church are to be subject to Him; and, as we have no way of ascertaining the mind of Christ except through the Scriptures, it follows that the affairs of the Church are to be managed by those officers whom the Lord Jesus has entrusted with that power, and are, without the interference of any external authority, to be regulated according to the mind of God as expressed in His Word.

CHAPTER THREE

Application of the Test

LET THE READER seriously consider the evidence submitted in the previous chapter, and we think he will be satisfied that there is Divine authority for saying that the principles, of which the following facts are the realisation, were in practical operation in the Apostolic Church:

(1) The office-bearers were chosen by the people.

(2) The office of bishop and elder was identical.

(3) There was a plurality of elders in each Church.

(4) Ordination was the act of a presbytery — that is, of a plurality of elders.

(5) There was the privilege of appeal to the assembly of elders; and the power of government was exercised by them in their associate capacity.

(6) The only Head of the Church was the Lord Jesus Christ.

The principles embodied in these six facts cover the whole platform of Church government, each rising in importance above that which precedes it, in an ascending series, from Popular Election up to the Headship of the Lord. We have been conducted to them, not by any process of wiredrawn logic, but by receiving the Scriptures, as we think every child of God should receive them, except there be manifest and good reasons to the contrary, in the plain, simple, and natural sense. The most unlettered reader, if he be only unprejudiced and honest, cannot examine the passages of Scripture we have specified, and fail to see that these six great principles were all embodied in the government of the Apostolic Church. But whether they are embodied in those forms of ecclesiastical government at present existing in the world is another and a very important question — a question which it is now our business to answer. We proceed, therefore, to bring the existing systems in succession to the test of the apostolic standard.

PRELACY

AS ALREADY EXPLAINED, Prelacy is that system of Church government which is dispensed by archbishops, bishops, priests, deans, deacons, and other office-bearers. It is exemplified in the Church of Rome and in the Church of England, both of which are prelatic in their government; the difference being, that the prelacy of Rome vests the ecclesiastical supremacy in the pope, while the prelacy of England vests it in the reigning monarch. With this exception, the two Churches, however widely they may differ in doctrine, are, in every important point of government, the same. As many may be disposed to consider the prelacy of a Protestant Church much less objectionable than the prelacy of Rome, and as we have neither necessity nor desire to take any unfair advantage in argument, we prefer to bring the prelacy of Protestantism into comparison with the apostolic standard.

The fountain of jurisdiction in the Church of England is the monarch for the time being, who inherits the throne by hereditary descent, and who, irrespective of all character, is by Act of Parliament, the only supreme head of the Church of England and Ireland (37 Henry VIII, chapter 17). No person can be received into the ministry of that Church till he subscribe this article: ''That the king's majesty, under God, is the only supreme governor of this realm, and of all other his highness' dominions and countries, *as well in all spiritual, or ecclesiastical things* or causes, as temporal'' (*Canon* 36). The appointment of all the arch-bishops and bishops is vested in the Crown, which is guided in the selection by the political administration of the day — a body composed of persons of every hue of religious profession, and only kept in its place by the majority of votes it can command in Parliament. The highest ecclesiastical office-bearers under the Crown are the archbishops, of whom there are two in England — the archbishops of Canterbury and York, and two in Ireland — the archbishops of Armagh and Dublin. Each of these has under him a number of suffragan bishops, and each bishop has under his care the inferior clergy of his diocese, who preach and dispense the ordinances of religion to such inhabitants of their parishes as are pleased to receive them. The parish clergy are, in some instances, appointed by the Crown, in others by the bishop, in others by a lay patron, and sometimes in a mode still more objectionable.

Such is Prelacy in its most favourable form, as presented in the Protestant Establishment of England. Let us compare it with the system of government which we have already ascertained to exist in the Apostolic Church.

In the Apostolic Church, the office-bearers were chosen by the people; but, in the Church of England, archbishops and bishops are chosen by the Crown, and the subordinate clergy are appointed to their charges either by the diocesan, or by some landed proprietor, or by some civil corporation. The people of the Apostolic Church exercised the privilege of electing an apostle; the people in the Church of England have not power to elect a curate.

In the Apostolic Church, the office of bishop and elder was identical; the elders of Ephesus were the bishops of the flock; but, in the Church Establishment, it is very different. The apostolic elder, being a teacher and ruler of a congregation, resembles more closely the parish clergyman than any other office-bearer in the Church of England. But it is very evident that, in that Church, a parish clergyman holds a position widely different from a bishop. The rector wields the jurisdiction of a parish; but the bishop governs a diocese, that usually includes a whole multitude of parishes. The one presides over a single congregation; the other, over many congregations. The one exercises authority over the laity, but a Church of England bishop is the ruler of a band of clergy. If, then, the parish clergyman corresponds to the presbyter or elder of apostolic times, it is very clear that, in the Establishment, the bishop and elder are not identical in office. In the Established Church every elder is subject to his bishop; but, in the Apostolic Church, every elder was a bishop himself.

In the Church of England each congregation is under the care of one presbyter. When a second is called in, he is a mere curate in the employment of another, and void of all ecclesiastical jurisdiction. It is not very common, and certainly not essential to the system, to have more than one presbyter or elder in each Church; whereas, we have seen that, in each Church of apostolic times, there was a plurality of elders.

In the Church of England ordination is an act exclusively performed by a prelate; he may ask others to unite with him, but it is his presence not theirs that is essential to the act: whereas, in the Apostolic Church, it was the practice to ordain men to the office of the ministry with the laying on of the hands of the presbytery.

In the Church of England, no matter what ecclesiastical grievance may exist, there is no power of appeal except to the courts of law, or the Queen's Privy Council, or some such tribunal. The practice is unknown in the denomination of bringing any matter for consideration before the assembly of elders for them to decide upon, in accordance with the apostles' word. But this, as we have seen, was the mode in which affairs were managed in the Apostolic Church.

In our Protestant Establishment the monarch is, by act of Parliament, head of the Church, and to the king or queen, as the case may be, the 37th Article informs us that "the chief government of all estates of the realm, whether they be ecclesiastical or civil, *in all causes,* doth appertain"; whereas, in apostolic times, the Church had no head but Jesus Christ.

We have thus examined and compared the two Churches as closely and candidly as it is possible for us to do, and we feel ourselves forced to the conclusion that, of the six great principles of ecclesiastical government that met in the Apostolic Church, there is not one embodied in the Prelacy of the Church of England. We infer, therefore, that, while that Church may be entitled to great respect as a human system, maintained by Act of Parliament, and numbering in its ranks many estimable people, there is no ground whatever for regarding it, in point of government, as an Apostolic Church. At the peril of excommunication we feel bound to declare our conviction that the government of the Church of England is repugnant to the Word of God.*

INDEPENDENCY

IT IS DIFFICULT to ascertain the particulars of ecclesiastical order approved by Independents, inasmuch as we are not aware that they have embodied their views of what the Scriptures teach on the subject in any common formula, and as every congregation, standing apart from every other, may differ sometimes widely on important points. We are, therefore, left to discover their views of Church polity from the general practices known to exist among them, and from the principles advocated by their most eminent writers. These, however, are sufficiently known to enable us to compare the Independent system of Church government with the apostolic standard.

The principle of popular election existed, as we have seen, in the Primitive Church, and had the sanction of the apostles of the Lord. Among the Independents this principle is preserved in its integrity: with them every ecclesiastical office-bearer is chosen by the people.

In the Apostolic Church the office of bishop and elder was identical; the bishop did not exercise any authority over the elder; on the contrary, every

---

* No. VII of the *Constitutions and Canons Ecclesiastical,* agreed upon with the king's license in 1603, and republished by the Prayer-Book and Homily Society (1852) is as follows: "Whosoever shall hereafter affirm, That the government of the Church of England under his majesty by archbishops, bishops, deans, archdeacons, and the rest that bear office in the same, is anti-Christian or repugnant to the Word of God; let him be excommunicated *ipso facto,* and so continue till he repent, and publicly revoke such his wicked errors."

bishop was an elder, and every elder a bishop. So it is with Independents. Every one of their pastors fills the office of bishop and elder, and none of them claims authority over others. With them a bishop and elder are only different names for the same office-bearers, as it was in apostolic days.

We have seen how, in apostolic times, there was a plurality of elders in each Church. Here the Independent system fails. On the principles of that theory of Church government, it is scarcely possible to have a plurality of elders, and in practice it rarely, if ever, occurs. Among them there is only one minister, or bishop, or elder, in each congregation. Practically, their system admits only of one elder to each Church. If an apostle were writing an epistle to an Independent Church, he would never think of addressing it to the *bishops,* as well as to the deacons, for the simple reason that, with them, there is usually but *one* bishop to one Church: nor could an apostle ever send for the *elders* of an Independent Church, as Paul sent for the elders of Ephesus, for the plain reason that, in an Independent Church, there is usually but one elder. A single pastor, with deacons under him, governing a Church, is the prominent feature that the Independent system everywhere presents — an arrangement than which none can be more opposed to the plurality of elders that existed in each congregation in primitive times. Some Independents attempt to palliate their departure from apostolic precedent, by saying that a plurality of elders is desirable, but their Churches are not able to support them. Does it never strike our esteemed brethren that there must be some remarkable disparity between the apostolic system and theirs, when the richest of their Churches now cannot afford to possess what was possessed by the very poorest Churches in the days of the apostles? It is the Word of God that says of Paul and Barnabas — "they ordained elders in *every* Church".

The office-bearers of the Apostolic Church were set apart to the discharge of their peculiar duties with the laying on of the hands of the presbytery. Among Independents, however, ordination of any sort is not essential; frequently it is counted unnecessary. Instances are known of persons acting as pastors of Churches for a lifetime, who were never inducted to office with the imposition of hands and prayer. Ordination is not required by the system. With them it is a mere matter of taste, left in each case to the individual choice. If the newly elected pastor choose to have himself ordained, it can only be done in a way inconsistent with Independent principles. The congregation, being destitute of a plurality of elders, his ordination can only come from the people, who have no Scriptural right to confer it, or from the neighbouring pastor. But who does not see that the latter practice is entirely at variance with the foundation principle of Independency, namely, that each congregation has *within* itself complete materials for government? So much is this felt to be the case, that while some ask the assistance of the pastors of the district on such occasions, those who choose to carry out their Congregationalist principle with a little more consistency make light of ordination, think it unnecessary, and prefer to go without it.

In the Apostolic Church there was the privilege of appeal to the assembly of elders. Among the Independents nothing of this kind can exist. The distinctive principle of their system precludes all appeal. The decision of the pastor, and deacons, and people, assembled in a Church meeting, is final in every case. No matter how partial or unjust their decision is felt to be, there is no power of bringing the sentence under review of a less prejudiced and more enlightened tribunal. The judgment of the Church may be in strict accordance with justice, or it may be the offspring of prejudice or malevolence in a few of the leaders of the meeting, masked, of course, under zeal for purity of communion, and for the cause of religion; but, no matter how superficial the investigation, or how deep the wrong, the system deprives the injured man of the privilege of appeal, and clothes the perpetrators with irresponsible power. By denying and repudiating all association, it enables the rulers to be, if they please, the tyrants of the Church, and strips the injured of the possibility of redress. "Independency," says Dr. Wardlaw, "is the *competency* of every distinct Church to manage, *without appeal,* its own affairs."* This is an ingenious mode of disguising the most repulsive feature of the system. Very few would deny that a Church is competent to manage its own affairs in such a way as to obviate the necessity of appeal; but what we assert is, that, when the Church lacks the necessary wisdom and discretion to do so, appeal among Independents is not permitted, the injured is deprived of redress, and power, for which the possessor is irresponsible to man, degenerates into tyranny when it is unwisely exercised, and there is nothing to keep it in check. The case of Antioch shows that, when a difference arose in the primitive Church, there was a right of referring the matter to the assembly of elders, who, under the guidance of the apostles, settled the business. Elders might still meet, and the written word of the apostles is accessible to all, and a decision pronounced by parties removed from the scene of controversy, untainted by local prejudices, and standing far away from the partisanship of the leaders, might go far now, as in ancient days, to calm dissensions, should they unfortunately arise. But Independents, in this respect, repudiate the apostolic example. Their principle is to refuse all recognition of external authority, to make the decision of the Church meeting final in every case, and to deny to them who are aggrieved the privilege of appeal.

The Headship of Christ was a principle of apostolic times. Independents, we are happy to say, acknowledge this principle in all its integrity.

The result of our comparison is, that there are three principles of the Apostolic Church that we find fully acknowledged and acted upon among our

---

* Dr. Wardlaw's *Congregational Independency*, page 232. Glasgow, 1848.

Independent brethren, namely, popular election, the identity of presbyter and bishop, and the Headship of Christ over the Church. But there are three apostolic principles that we fail to find in their system, namely, the plurality of elders in each Church, ordination with the laying on of the hands of the presbytery, and the privilege of appeal. We conclude, therefore, that, while the Independent system of government advances to the pattern of primitive times much more closely than that which exists in the Churches of England and Rome, still it is not the system entitled to plead the precedent of the Apostolic Church.

PRESBYTERIANISM

IT ONLY NOW REMAINS that we compare the Presbyterian system with the standard of the law and of the testimony. The term *Presbyterian* is derived from the word *presbytery,* because the leading characteristic of this form of Church government is, that it entrusts the duty of ruling the Church to the presbytery — that is, to the presbyters or elders of the Church in their assembled capacity. But let us bring it, as well as the others, to the Scriptural standard.

In the Apostolic Church, we have mentioned frequently already, that popular election was an admitted principle. It is so with Presbyterians. In all Presbyterian Churches throughout Britain and America, with the single exception of the Established Church of Scotland, the members of each congregation invariably elect their own office-bearers. The privilege has been sometimes abused, as what good thing has not been abused by the sin and infatuation of man? But it is a Scriptural privilege that the Apostolic Church bequeaths us, and Presbyterians have often shown that they count it more precious than gold.

In the primitive age, the office of bishop and elder was identical. An elder was not inferior, in point of official standing, to a bishop, nor a bishop to an elder. It is so in the Presbyterian Church. Every elder is a bishop, or overseer of the flock; and every bishop is an elder, one whose office is to rule in the house of God. There are two departments in the office of the elder — that of teaching, and that of ruling; but the office itself is one.

There was a plurality of elders or bishops in each congregation of the Apostolic Church. Such is the practice in every Presbyterian Church at the present day. There is in each of their congregations a number of persons ordained to the office of the eldership, one of whom at least gives himself to the work of the ministry in its various departments, particularly that of public instruction, while the others give their principal attention to ruling in the Church of God. Teaching and ruling, as we have already stated, are different departments of the same office; and, while there can be no doubt that those appointed to the office have, in the abstract, a right to fill both departments, yet, in practice, it is found more convenient and beneficial for the people that each elder give most of his attention to that department whose duties he is best qualified to discharge. All elders, being bishops, have an equal right, according to the Scriptures, to preach, baptise, administer the Lord's Supper, and ordain*, but these duties it is arranged to devolve on one of the elders, called by distinction the *minister,* who is specially trained to his work, and is, by general consent, admitted to possess most gifts and attainments, and who, in consequence, is the best qualified to make these ordinances edifying to the Church; while the majority of the elders only rule, visit the sick, superintend Sabbath Schools, conduct prayer meetings, and make themselves useful in other ways. Presbyterians, therefore, maintain a plurality of elders in every Church; and, as it was in apostolic days, it is customary among them for elders to rule who do not labour in word and doctrine. Any unprejudiced person may see from 1 Timothy 5:17, that the office of the eldership divided itself into two great departments of duty in primitive times, even as at present. "Let the elders that rule well be counted worthy of double honour, especially they who labour in the word and doctrine." Dr. King's comment on this text must, for sense and truthfulness, commend itself to every intelligent man: "These words," he says, "could suggest to an unbiased reader only one meaning, that all elders who rule well are worthy of abundant honour, but especially those of their number who, besides ruling well, also labour in word and doctrine. Of course, the passage so interpreted, bears that, of the elders who rule well, only some labour in word and doctrine — that is, there are ruling elders, and among these teaching elders, as we have at the present day."† We are tempted thus to insert the true exposition of this celebrated passage, of which we have been often charged by our opponents as giving interpretations the most grotesque and extravagant. But the reader is requested to observe that the point which we have particularly in view at present is, that the Presbyterian, like the Apostolic Church, has, in every congregation, a plurality of elders.

Office-bearers were set apart to their distinct spheres of duty in the Apostolic Church with the laying on of the hands of the presbytery. The Presbyterian Church, in its several branches, is the only one known to us that carries this Scriptural principle invariably into practice.

In the Apostolic Church there was recognised the privilege of appeal and the right of government. This privilege is not only admitted, but it is one of the most distinguishing principles of Presbyterianism. Should any difference arise in a

---

* It is to be understood that in the Presbyterian Church it is only those licensed and ordained by the Presbytery to the office of the Ministry who may administer the Sacraments.

† King, op. cit., page 115.

congregation, the members are competent to settle the matter without appeal, if they please; but, should this fail, it is equally competent for them to refer the whole matter, either for advice or decision, to the assembly of elders met in presbytery. The highest ecclesiastical court known to the system is the *Presbytery;* the *Synod* being the name usually given to the presbytery of a province, and the *General Assembly* being the name that convenience has attached to the presbytery of a nation. The General Assembly has jurisdiction over a Synod only because it is a larger presbytery. Hence, that *subordination of Church Courts,* which some injudicious friends of Presbyterianism speak of as being a main feature of the system, is a mere accidental arrangement, which experience has proved conducive to union and strength, but which is by no means essential to the existence of the system. This is proved by the fact that a denomination, without either Synod or Assembly, and possessing no Church court whatever except a district presbytery, is, nevertheless, a complete Presbyterian body. Let there be only one assembly of elders to which a congregation can submit an appeal, and the apostolic principle is preserved. It is not even certain that *representation* is a main feature of the system, although a virtual representation is the result of existing arrangements. There is representation so far as that a few office-bearers, chosen by the people on their first admission to office, transact business for the many. Nor are all office-bearers privileged to find admission to the higher courts; for, although all elders are, in the abstract, equal in point of official power, and have, of course, equal right to sit in presbytery, yet, for convenience sake, it has been agreed upon that only a part of them shall at the same time exercise this right. In the Presbyterian Church of Ireland, it has been the immemorial custom, and long experience has only served to confirm its advantages, for two elders, the teaching elder or minister, and a ruling elder, to take their seats in presbytery. The result of these arrangements is, that a virtual representation occurs, and the system enjoys all its advantages; but to say it is a main pillar of Presbyterianism is contrary, in our opinion, to the facts of the case. Were the platform of the presbytery so widened as to give every elder a seat in our Church courts, this would, in a great measure, do away with representation, and would be unwise for many reasons, but would not shake a pillar of the system. In the meantime, whatever may be thought of the principle of representation and the subordination of Church courts, there can be no doubt that the Presbyterian form of government, in common with that of the Apostolic Church, secures to the people the *right of appeal to the assembly of elders, and grants to the assembly of elders the right of government* — a privilege which, so far as known to us, is enjoyed by no denomination that is not, in point of government, Presbyterian.

In the Apostolic Church, the Lord Jesus alone was King and Head. This is a truth acknowledged by all Presbyterians, and practically acted upon by all, except a very few, who, owing to their connection with the State, have been charged with a virtual departure from the principle. All Presbyterian Churches rank among their most cherished, as well as distinctive principles, that *Christ alone is King and Head of His Church.* As a denomination, Presbyterians have ever held that the Church, independent of the civil rulers, has supreme jurisdiction in all spiritual matters, and that its office-bearers are bound to exercise that jurisdiction in conformity to the mind of Christ, as expressed in His Word. The doctrine of the Supreme Headship of Jesus Christ over His Church is one to which Presbyterians have always been warm in their attachment.

We find, then, on minute and patient examination, that the six main principles of government that were, by inspired men established in the Apostolic Church, are all recognised and practically carried out among Presbyterians. We know no other denomination in the world, of whose form of ecclesiastical government the same statement could be made without departure from the truth.

THE RESULT

HERE, THEN, is the result of our investigations and comparisons. The Word of God contains six great, well-defined principles of government, that were embodied in that Church which was planted and organised by the inspired apostles of the Lord. All existing modern Churches claim to be apostolic, and, with the exception of the Greek and Roman Churches, profess to adopt the Scriptures as the sole rule of faith and practice. But, on comparing the prelacy of the Church of England with the standard of the Divine Word, it is found that in that Church not one of the apostolic principles of government is recognised or embodied. Among the Independents, three of the apostolic principles are exemplified in practice; the remaining three are nowhere to be found. Among Presbyterians, these six principles are all acknowledged, and every one of them is a main feature of the Presbyterian system. We now remind the reader of the axiom with which we entered on the investigation: *The modern Church which embodies in its government most apostolic principles, comes nearest in its government to the Apostolic Church.* We apply this axiom to the settlement of the case. Our conclusion is, that, while the prelacy of Rome and England is in direct opposition to the form of ecclesiastical government that was sanctioned by inspired men; and while Independency approaches much more nearly, but still falls short of the primitive model, *the Presbyterian is, in point of government, the only Apostolic Church.*

We are, indeed, very far from maintaining that any Church on earth is *in everything* an exact model of the pattern presented in the primitive age. It requires very little thought to see that the Apostolic Church of the Scriptures is altogether unique — one that in *all its parts* is never to be realised in this world again. There were in it apostles, prophets, and apostolic delegates — all vested with extraordinary powers, which have been handed down to no successors. It was quite common for the early preachers to work miracles in confirmation of their doctrine, and confer the Holy Ghost by the laying on of their hands. Sometimes in the same congregation there were several gifted brethren, who could look into the future with prophetic eye and declare infallibly the mind of God. In the Church of Jerusalem, organised by the whole college of apostles, and the mother of all other churches, there was a community of goods established; and it was quite a common thing for the people of those days, when their hearts were warm with the first glow of love to the Lord Jesus, to sell their property, and lay the price of it at the apostles' feet. There were no public buildings erected for the celebration of Christian worship during all the apostolic age; and public teachers, instead of confining the labours of a life to one little district in the country, went everywhere preaching the Word. These are matters as to which no sect that we know of has been able yet to copy the Apostolic Church, or is ever very likely to do so.

Again, there are some arrangements, some of them very unimportant, interwoven with the Presbyterian system, for which it would be difficult to find precedent in the Scriptures. We have already adverted to *representation* — the practice of one or two elders representing their brother elders in our meetings of presbytery — an arrangement founded more on common sense than Scripture, and adopted to prevent any individual congregation from exercising a preponderance of influence, and to secure, as far as possible, calm deliberation and impartial sentences. Could we command in the assembly of elders the personal presence of inspired apostles to guide the brethren to a right decision, we are sure all would go well, and we might not be so solicitous as to representation; but, so long as humanity falls short of perfection, it is right to guard against abuses, and to impose upon the exercise of arbitrary power a salutary check. There is no plan better adapted to accomplish this, and to secure at the same time the confidence of the people, than that of representation. We have also spoken of the subordination of church courts, an arrangement entered into for giving effect to the principle of appeal, and which not only gives to the denomination unity and strength, but is obviously attended with many other advantages. The utility of both these principles is undoubted, but it were vain to say that they are essentials of Presbyterianism.

It is not uncommon to hear people speak of the advantages that accrue to the Presbyterian system from the admittance of the *lay* element into Church courts.

This must be a misunderstanding altogether. None but elders — teaching and ruling elders — are competent to sit in any Presbyterian Church court, from the session of a congregation up to the General Assembly, and, as we have already seen, all elders are equal in point of official standing, for though their departments of duty are in some respects different, yet the office is one and the same. No elder of any kind is a *layman,* but an ecclesiastical office-bearer, ordained with the laying on of the hands of the presbytery, and appointed to the oversight of the flock and to the discharge of spiritual duties. Nor does an elder sit in our Church courts to represent the laity. He represents the laity in no sense different from that in which the minister represents them; both are chosen by the people, and both fill the one office in the Church, the only difference between them being one of education, of labour, and of reward. The notion is only plausible from the fact that most elders are engaged in secular pursuits. But it should be remembered that all ministers were so engaged at the first. Even an apostle lived by his trade, as he repeatedly informs us (Acts 20:34; 18:3; 1 Corinthians 4:12; 1 Thessalonians 2:9; 2 Thessalonians 3:8); and it was part of Paul's charge to the bishops of Ephesus, "that *so labouring* they ought to support the weak" (Acts 20:35). If the pursuit of secular employments proves our elders to be laymen — then the bishops of Ephesus were laymen, and the Apostle of the Gentiles was a layman too. It is equally in vain to argue that, as the brethren were present in the apostolic council (Acts 15:23), the laity are entitled to be represented, and are represented by the elders in our Church courts; for, as every one knows, elders and brethren were both present in that council, and therefore the one could not represent the other — each class had a place and a function of its own. Elders sit in their own right as spiritual rulers in the house of God. There are in our Church courts no *lay* representatives and no *lay elders* — a name which ignorance invented and malevolence has preserved, in order to bring the office into contempt and disrepute.

It is, however, only candid to say that such grotesque notions of ecclesiastical order, as these terms betray, have received countenance from the disparity that in the course of time has risen between the elders who teach and the elders who rule. This disparity is not the result of any ecclesiastical enactment, but was at the beginning, and still is, the effect mainly of a difference of gifts. The most gifted of the elders was in the beginning set to preach, and what at first was only a difference of gifts has grown in the progress of time to wear the appearance of a difference of rank. One is here reminded of the truthful remark of Dr. Campbell: "Power has a sort of attractive force, which gives it a tendency to accumulate, insomuch that what in the beginning is a distinction barely perceptible, grows in process of time a most remarkable disparity."

The disparity existing among teaching and ruling elders among Presbyterians, instead of being defended, is very much to be lamented, and ought as much as possible to be removed. This is to be done, however, not by lowering the teaching elder, but by elevating the ruling elder, and appointing to office those only who are distinguished from the people by more than a common measure of graces and gifts, who are aware of the responsibilities of the eldership, and who are determined, for the Lord's sake, to the best of their ability to discharge its duties. Besides, the office of the deacon, existing at present only in some congregations, should be revived in every Church, where elders can manage temporal matters only by neglecting the spiritual concerns peculiarly their own. These and other defects can be remedied, when once they are seen to be defects; for it is one among the many recommendations of the Presbyterian Church polity, that it possesses within itself a purifying and reforming power, by which, while always preserving the Scriptural and essential principles of the system, it can alter any arrangement that experience has proved in its practical operation not to be productive of good.

We do not, then, assert that the Presbyterian Church is in everything an exact copy of the Apostolic Church. There are some things found in the one that must be for ever wanting in the other; and conversely, there are some things wanting in the one that are found in the other. But in doctrine they are exactly the same: in worship they are exactly the same: in government, all the main principles of the one are found in the other. There is no other Church on earth of which the same statements can be made in truth. We regard it, therefore, as put beyond all reasonable doubt, *that of all the Churches now existing in the world, the Presbyterian Church comes nearest to the model of apostolic times.* That such is the fact, every man, who gives to the evidence here submitted that careful and unprejudiced consideration to which it is entitled, must, as we think, be convinced.

CHAPTER FOUR

Practical Lessons

THE APOSTOLIC PRINCIPLES of Church government are the peculiarities of the Presbyterian system. That other Churches neither practise nor acknowledge these principles, is the main ground why Presbyterians remain separate from them.

I know of no good reason for my being a Presbyterian rather than an Independent, except that I believe Presbyterianism has done what the rival system has failed to do — preserved the principles of apostolic government; and, for this reason, possesses an amount of Scriptural warrant (not to speak of unity, coherence, and vigour), that Independency can never have. The absence of these apostolic principles in the Prelatic Establishment must always keep enlightened and conscientious Presbyterians out of its pale, no matter what be the modifications introduced into its articles, or what change be wrought upon its ritual.

If our distinctive principles are not apostolic and important, Presbyterianism is not only folly, but very great folly; and, by standing apart from other denominations upon such a ground, we only perpetuate needless divisions in the Church of God. If we discover that the peculiarities of the system are either not true, or truths of minor consequence, we should take speedy steps to heal the schism that exists, and exemplify Christian union on a large scale by uniting with some sister sect, whose principles are more Scriptural and important than our own. But if, on the other hand, our distinctive principles are very important as well as true, then duty to God and the Church demands that we avow, illustrate, and defend them, and press them on the notice of the world.

In discharging either of these duties, Presbyterians at present seem rather remiss. As a denomination we show no desire to renounce our distinctive principles, and merge into Prelacy or Independency; nor, on the other hand, do we make such efforts to teach and propagate them as the truth has a right to expect at our hands. By deriving the name and character of our ecclesiastical system from these principles, we seem to tell the world that they are of very great importance; by our habitual reserve on this topic in our pulpit ministrations, we seem to say that they are of very little. Our conduct is in this respect ambiguous and vacillating. We construct with the one hand, and demolish with the other. On the ground of certain principles we keep apart from other sects; and yet to teach these principles from the pulpit is usually viewed as an intrusion inconsistent with the Gospel. Our separate existence as a Church clothes our pecularities with consequence; our habitual forgetfulness of impressing them upon the people, deepens, if it does not produce, the popular notion that they are of no consequence whatever.

That expositions of our principles are very rarely delivered from the pulpit, is a fact that few acquainted with the circumstances of the case will venture to deny. I sat myself for years in various Presbyterian Churches of town and country; I never failed to hear the Gospel of Christ, and the great precepts of Christian morality preached by our ministers, and enforced always with great faithfulness, and sometimes with considerable power; but I do not remember to have ever heard on any occasion, except at the settlement of a minister, any attempt made to teach the people why they should be Presbyterians and not Prelatists — and yet I never worshipped where there was not a parish church within a distance of two miles. I have met with not a few others, who tell me they have sat all their lives in Presbyterian Churches, and do not remember to have heard on any Sabbath a single principle of Presbyterian Church polity stated and explained. The *Plea of Presbytery,* one of the very ablest defences of Apostolic Church government and worship that the present century has produced, testifies to the singular fact of the silence of the pulpit on our distinctive principles. In the preface to their volume, the authors of that work make the following observations: "Can he (Mr. Boyd) point to a single Presbyterian minister *in Ulster,* who had previously addressed a congregation for four successive Sabbaths on the peculiarities of Presbyterianism? Can he name a Presbyterian minister who had previously employed a single Sabbath in the discussion of the subject? *We are satisfied that he cannot plead even one such case* as an apology for his agitation of the controversy." To all this there may be some honourable exceptions; but still it cannot be fairly denied that the exposition of our Church polity has, in general, become unfashionable and unusual. Even at ordinations, the explanation of our principles is beginning to be felt as a periodical encumbrance — inconsistent with the liberality of modern times — which immemorial custom has entailed upon us; and good easy people, who wish, at any price, to stand well with their neighbours, and fear to give offence by telling honest truth, desire to have the discourse on Presbyterianism, customary on such occasions, either entirely abolished, or, what amounts to the same thing, so softened down as to please everybody. And from the press an exposition of Presbyterian principles rarely issues, except when some champion of another sect, animated by our apathy, is brave enough to attack our system; and then some Presbyterian warrior, clad in the panoply of battle, descends into the field of controversy; but before he strikes a blow, he takes care to apologise for his intrusion upon the public, by alleging that he appears in self-defence — which is much the same as saying that he would not have troubled the world by telling it the truth had he not been provoked by the occasion. This candid avowal prepares the reader, at the very commencement, to regard the warmth of the writer's zeal as only an ebullition of personal resentment, and the keenest thrusts of his logic as only the envenomed stings of sectarian retaliation.

The causes of this guilty silence are manifold. I do not believe that we are ashamed of our Presbyterianism, and yet it seems very much as if it were so. The fact, however, is, that some ministers never have had their attention particularly directed to the vast importance of making their people familiar with the grounds on which Presbyterians stand separate from other Christians; and a knowledge of which every reflecting mind must see is so necessary to produce consistency of conduct, and to perpetuate our denominational existence. Others keep silent, because to betray strong attachment to Presbyterian principles seems bigoted and uncharitable, and interferes too rudely with the evangelical heresy so popular in our day — that all forms of the Protestant religion are equally true and equally deserving the support and encouragement of Christians. But the main cause of the silence of the pulpit on the subject is the impression so prevalent among the ministry, that our distinctive principles are so clearly written in the Scriptures as to be evident to all, and that, therefore, the public advocacy of Presbyterianism is unnecessary. This, I am persuaded, is a clerical delusion, gross and gigantic. Presbyterian principles are, indeed, clearly embodied in the Bible, but we are not to forget that what is very clear to one man may be very dark to another. The popular mind, so acute in the business of everyday life, is but a dull learner in the things of God, and at every step needs help and guidance, in order that it may reach right views on spiritual matters. Clearly as Presbyterianism is written in the Scriptures, I consider the Gospel to be written there still more clearly; and yet it is no uncommon thing to meet people familiar with the sound of the Bible from childhood, and clergymen whose business is to preach it, and authors who have attempted to instruct the world on religion, who are all alike ignorant of the main principles of the Gospel of Christ. As it would not be wise for the Preacher of the Cross to leave the multitude to discover in the Bible the Gospel for themselves, so it is not wise to leave them without assistance in their search for Presbyterianism. One a very little more advanced in knowledge than ourselves can, in a few minutes, show us meaning in a passage of Scripture that we never saw in it before, and can leave us wondering why we read it so often, and never viewed it till that moment in a light so beautiful and true. Besides, it seems clear that, if Church government is a portion of the revealed will of God, duty demands that from every faithful minister it should receive, in the prelections of the pulpit, a place proportioned to its importance. There is peculiar need, moreover, that, in this department, the people should receive the assistance of the minister; for, in dealing with the apostolic system, there is an amount of labour in the collection of passages, in the comparison of facts, and in the deduction of inferences, that few minds, left to their own unaided efforts, are zealous enough to engage, and vigorous enough to accomplish. And whose duty is it to supply help, if not his, who is called by the Holy Ghost, and chosen by the voice of the people, to labour in word and doctrine? "The priest's lips should keep knowledge, and they should seek the law at his mouth."

Whatever be the cause of the silence of the pulpit on the distinctive principles of the Presbyterian system, the sad results of it are manifest every day. The intelligent few who have attained to some acquaintance with our principles, have derived their knowledge from the Bible and from books, very seldom from the pulpit; while the many, being uninformed on such subjects, act sometimes in open violation of them. Multitudes frequent the meeting-house, because they have been accustomed to do so from childhood, not because they have ever thought of the peculiar principles of the Presbyterian system, and from an examination of the Word of God are satisfied of their truth. They are Presbyterians by birth and habit only, very seldom by conviction. Not being systematically taught that the principles of government operating in their own Church are exclusively apostolic, many of the Presbyterian people appear to regard all Protestant Churches as standing upon the same level of truth; they do not trouble themselves with forms of faith; in their view the Westminster Confession and the Thirty-nine Articles are only facsimiles of each other; Prelacy, Independency, and Presbytery are all alike to them — it is only bigotry that pretends to see a difference. Opinions of this sort are now so common that no odium attaches to their profession, and are vastly popular, especially with rich Presbyterians, who ape at fashion, and meditate at some early day renegadism to the Establishment. Nor is it very wonderful that many others, untaught to consider Presbyterian principles as a portion of Divine revelation, and surrounded by many circumstances tending to deepen the impression that all forms of the Protestant faith are equally Scriptural, are kept in the Church only by the force of habit, or personal attachment to some worthy minister, and are ready to fling the nominal profession of apostolic principles away from them, so soon as the time comes that a secession from the Presbyterian Church can advance their worldly interests, please their superiors, feed their revenge, or gratify a whim.

There can be little doubt that ignorance of the Scriptural truth and practical value of our principles, has made the Presbyterian community much colder to their own Church than otherwise they would be. I have often remarked how a Roman Catholic, a Methodist, a Baptist — each thinks his own Church the purest and best in the world; while a Presbyterian is usually a man who regards any other Protestant Church as being at the very least as good as his own. It is this popular persuasion that in Ulster lends proselytism all its power. Some of the smaller sects endeavour to diffuse the impression that the differences between Protestant Churches are of no consequence, and it is their interest to do so; they have little to lose and much to gain by such an impression being abroad. Every minister among them who knows his business is, of course, a vigorous, and doubtless a conscientious supporter of the Evangelical Alliance. The prelatic clergy also, except in some rare case, do their best to diffuse the same feeling among Dissenters, because it gives them freer access to convey their Puseyism into Presbyterian families; and because, being wise in their generation, they have the sagacity to see that, when the Presbyterian mind becomes saturated with the feeling, that there is no difference between the two Churches, the question will soon follow — Why tax ourselves for nothing; why be at the expense of supporting a separate Church; why not join the Establishment? If proselytism gives us any annoyance, we have none but ourselves to blame. Were we faithful to our own principles, the people would be faithful to us. The prevalent indifference to Presbyterianism that our defective instruction has produced, has left us open to the incursions of every sect that chooses to give us opposition, and which, in so doing, may always safely reckon on the countenance and co-operation of some of ourselves. It has turned the Presbyterian Church of Ireland into a sort of ecclesiastical preserve, where foot of Papist dare not trespass, but where every marksman, who wears the mask of Protestanism, is free to sport at pleasure and to bag his game. Let the blame be all our own, if the thoughtless among our people are, from time to time, taken in the snare of the fowler.

Instead, however, of pouring forth unavailing regrets over past deficiencies, perhaps it were well for all of us to consider the most likely expedient for communicating a new and better tone to the Presbyterian mind. This the ministry have it in their power to do the very moment that they *will* it. The clergy of no other denomination are able to wield over intelligent society an influence equal to ours. The General Assembly comprises the assembled ministers of the kingdom, and a great master mind, taking advantage of his position in the house to write some great truths on the hearts of his audience, can given an impulse to a principle that is felt to the very extremities of the nation. Like the sons of youth, each auditor there is an arrow in the hands of a mighty man. The sentiments and principles there enunciated are conveyed by each minister to his respective sphere of labour; and in his hands sentiment becomes embodied in action. Scattered at due intervals over all parts of the kingdom, our ministers are each the centre of a circle peculiarly his own; they come into contact with society at all points, from the highest to the lowest in the scale of intelligence; they address the people publicly at least once or twice a week the whole year round, and they go forth to hold private intercourse with every family at its own fireside; they take part in public meetings, preside over the education of youth, contribute to newspapers and magazines, and have access, in many other different ways, to the intellects and hearts of the people. It is needless to add that this gives us vast influence for good or for evil. We have it in our power to mould the opinions of our own community, and to make deep impression on society beyond. We have only to be unanimous for a principle, and advocate it with enthusiasm, in order to fasten that principle very deeply in the intellect of the kingdom. There is as much mind in the Presbyterian ministry at this moment as, if wisely directed, could revolutionise the religious sentiment of the nation.

Premising these things, it is obvious we have only to enter vigorously on a new line of action, in order to turn the tide of popular feeling completely in favour of Presbyterianism. It is never to be forgotten that, as ministers of the Gospel, there is deposited in our hands a very important trust. The duties of this trust are best discharged by each man striving to cultivate, to the utmost extent possible, that portion of the vineyard committed to his individual care. Zeal in other matters never can make up for deficiency in this. Let our ministers continue, as at present, to preach the Gospel faithfully, and to maintain that soundness in the faith, without which there can be no religious prosperity. Let them continue to exemplify in their own life and character that pure morality which they inculcate upon others. Let them redouble, if it be possible to redouble, their attention to the people, and spare no pains to carry the message of life to every fireside. Let them visit the sick, comfort them that mourn, instruct the ignorant, sympathise with the poor and oppressed, encourage missions, and lend a helping hand to every scheme that has for its object the promotion of benevolence and virtue. Let them, in everything, study to show themselves approved unto God — workmen that need not to be ashamed. But let them be assured that they neither serve the Church nor serve themselves, if they do not, by pulpit exposition and private instruction, use their efforts to engrave deeply on the minds of the people the distinctive principles of the Presbyterian system. I am far from saying that these things should be substituted for the Gospel of Christ; but, as we believe they form an integral portion of Divine revelation, it is our duty, as faithful ministers of Christ, to teach them to the people. I do not mean that any denomination should be systematically assailed in a bitter and an unchristian spirit; but it seems to me that, if a preacher only prophesy smooth things, preach only what he considers palatable to his audience, spare errors that are abroad in the community working much evil, and purposely keep back any portion of the truth for fear of being pronounced sectarian and uncharitable, he ceases to be the minister of God and becomes the servant of man. So long as we stand separate from the Establishment, it is no less our interest than our duty to make the Presbyterian people thoroughly acquainted with our reasons for maintaining and perpetuating a distinct ecclesiastical existence. Let our dissent rest upon the intelligence, not upon the ignorance, of the people; and instantly it becomes rational and consistent, and of course more formidable than ever. Personal attachment to a minister is a tie too weak to bind a people to the Church; for death or a removal may snap it asunder any day. The bonds of custom, kindred, and early association, though in some instances powerful enough, are not too strong to be broken, as experience often shows. It remains that we teach our congregations that our principles, forming, as they do, a portion of the Word of God, should be to all God's people, precious as gold. We should instruct them periodically as to what Presbyterianism is. Let each minister do this as mildly as he pleases, but let it be done faithfully and firmly. Let him not be turned from his purpose by the murmurs of disaffected parties within, or the clamours of enemies without, remembering that the patient cries most loudly when the physician probes the sore. Let him leave no man in doubt that he himself believes the principles of which he is the public representative, and that they are very dear to his heart. Let him take no steps tending to spread the popular error that our distinctive principles are trifles. While careful not to oppose other Christians who aim to advance the glory of God in their own way, he should neither aid nor encourage persons who systematically repudiate what we regard as great and important truths. And let him not fear to be called a bigot, for what is a *bigot* but the bad name which the world gives a man who ventures to have principles, and is firm enough to show through life a consistent attachment to them? In a word, the aim of all of us should be to make every man who is a Presbyterian by name a Presbyterian by conviction.

The lukewarm and odious indifference to Presbyterian principles that in this day meets one everywhere, calls loudly for a remedy of some kind. The best I know is from the text-book of the Divine Word to teach the people publicly and privately what Presbyterianism really is. Had we entered into one vast conspiracy to let our principles die out of the memory of the world, we could not adopt any course more likely to accomplish our end than never to breathe them from the pulpit. But if we wish the people to know and value them, it is very plain we must show that we know and value them ourselves. If we would drive any principles into the popular mind, and make them as "nails fastened by the master of assemblies", we must never cease to hammer at them. Sentiments perpetually falling from the pulpit, the platform, and the press, cannot, in the course of nature, for ever fall pointless to the earth; they may at first be disliked by not a few, but they will modify the views even of persons whose judgments have already attained maturity — they will fasten with the greatest tenacity on young minds opening to thought — they will spread abroad in ever-enlarging circles — they will grow to be public opinion at the last. The pulpit is the proper sphere for the promulgation of religious truth. Error needs no effort to spread it through the world, even as the seeds of nature, carried by the autumn wind, are sown broadcast over the land, and germinate in the soil without the culture of the husbandman; but truth rarely goes forth alone — the human heart has no natural affection for it — ignorance and prejudice obstruct its progress at every step — it requires an impulsive force to carry it though the world. Weeds grow of themselves, but the flower requires all the skill and care that the gardener can give it. Error sprouts rankly in human bosoms without any help of ours; but truth needs some kind hand to plant and water it, and keep it in the sunshine. Religious truth, of all others, presents least charms to the natural mind — and how truth of this nature can be expected to make its way through such a world as ours, without receiving an impetus from the pulpit, I do not know — I cannot even imagine. It is certain that a man who, at the proper time and place, states and illustrates his principles, and satisfies others that he believes and prizes them himself, is sure, sooner or later, to make converts to his views; but a man who is known to profess opinions, and is always silent on them, raises doubts as to his own sincerity, and never makes one.

If we wish to have Presbyterianism the religion of the Church universal, we must let the world know that we cherish a warm and devoted attachment to its principles. We should not halt between two opinions, clinging to one sect and giving our influence to another. We should cease to be a lukewarm and hybrid generation — Presbyterians only in name. This is not a time for inconsistency and doubt — but for decision, for energy, for action. Presbyterianism should be on the move. Every hour we delay to enter on some vigorous course of policy, our interests, as a denomination, suffer. In our circumstances, hesitation and inaction are fraught with danger, if not denominational death. Every pulpit we can command in the kingdom should strike instantly to a high Presbyterian key. If, as a denomination, we would be faithful to the truth of God; if we would have the people to understand and to love our system; if we would marshal public opinion against renegadism, and hold it up to contumely and scorn; if we would push our Presbyterianism, and call the attention of our fellow Christians to its Scripturality and its vigour; if we would have our friends to follow, and our enemies to fear us — then we should learn to regard our distinctive principles as our pride and glory, and preach and teach them, till the people know them like the alphabet, and an unwilling world be compelled to listen. The Church that forgets to assert and teach her peculiar principles lives in such a world as this only by sufferance; her own children are cold to her; and when she sinks to dust, she shall have few to lament her fall. But the Church that thunders its opinions in the ears of mankind, and which neither force nor flattery can silence, is a Church that will have many bitter enemies, but many warm friends — it will have many to hate, but it will have some to love, and some to die for it — it may be everywhere spoken against, but faithful to the truth of God, it will have saints and martyrs, and, in due time, bring the world to its feet.

A word, in conclusion, to the Presbyterian people. This little book is sent to the world principally on your account, that you may know the Scriptural grounds on which the Presbyterian form of Church government rests, and how its claims to apostolicity are so far superior to those of any rival system. I, at first, engaged in the study of the subject for my own personal profit and satisfaction, it afterwards occurred to me that a line of argument, which to me seems so clear and convincing, might be serviceable to others, who are anxious, as I was, to know the mind of Christ on this much controverted subject. I entered on the investigation with considerable misgivings, lest it should turn out that the system of ecclesiastical government with which I am connected is not divine in its origin. These misgivings were mainly produced by the plausible representations and confident assertions of Independent writers; and I do acknowledge that, had I given ear to their bravadoes, without consulting the Scriptures for myself, I must have ceased to be a Presbyterian. But with me it has ever been a principle to call no man *master,* and to take my opinions on religious matters from the Word of God alone. I sought light from the Fountain of Light. I asked the guidance of the Divine Spirit. I went directly to the Word of God, compared one passage with another, and endeavoured to arrive at apostolic principles. I brought the existing systems of Church government into juxtaposition with the Bible, and examined them in the light that shines from the Lamp of God. Lest any important passage of Scripture, or any weighty argument might escape my notice, I read some of the most plausible attacks ever made on Presbytery, and I have studied Prelacy and Independency as presented in the pages of the very ablest of their advocates. The result is, that I am persuaded Prelacy is a human system altogether — from top to bottom a fabric constructed by men. I am satisfied that Independency, in so far as it differs from Presbyterianism, is not so erroneous as it is defective; and that it stands in need of someone to "set in order the things that are wanting". I am, also, fully convinced that the

Presbyterian form of Church government approaches more closely than any other to that which existed in the Apostolic Church. To do full justice to all the arguments that might be advanced in favour of this system of ecclesiastical polity, would require a large book; but, as large books are often written but seldom read, I thought it better to go directly to the root of the matter, present you with the Scriptural view of the subject, and enable you to judge for yourselves. I have throughout studied to be brief, that you may have time to read, and plain, that the very humblest of you may understand. I have purposely shunned all elaborate discussion and intricate argumentation, and have tried to present you with facts from the Word of God bearing on the case — leading the reader by the hand to that pure fountain, and permitting him to draw water for himself. I now invite you to view in all its parts the evidence here submitted; examine if I have misquoted a text, falsified a fact, distorted a testimony, or taken the Scriptures in any other than their plain and natural sense; put the reasoning here presented to the very severest test that in fairness and honesty you can apply; give the statements of the Divine Word the weight to which they are justly entitled, and I am confident you will come to think with me that all the apostolic principles of ecclesiastical government are found in the Presbyterian Church alone. It is something to you, surely, to have good reasons for knowing that that Church, with whose ordinances the thoughts of your childhood are entwined — within whose temples beloved friends, now in heaven, learned the way of salvation, and were taught the lessons of life — and whose psalms and services are fragrant with the memory of martyrs, is, in its government, no less than its doctrine and worship, founded on, and agreeable to, the Word of God. Satisfied of this, it is your duty through life to give it a cordial and consistent support, to attend upon its sanctuaries, receive its lessons, and take your part in the various departments of usefulness which it presents. There is such a thing as being a Presbyterian without being a Christian, as it is possible to be a Christian without being a Presbyterian. Depend upon it, it is best to be both. Make the atonement of Christ the refuge of your souls; hold fast by every truth of God's Word, small and great; lend no encouragement to opposing errors; take no pains to conceal your attachment to Presbyterian principles; and strive to do honour to the system with which you claim connection, by your love to Christ, by an upright and consistent life, and by earnest endeavours on your part to deserve the character which distinguished the saints of God in other and better days — "a peculiar people, zealous of good works".

Westminster Confession of Faith

CHAPTER 31 — OF SYNODS AND COUNCILS

I. For the better government, and further edification of the Church, there ought to be such assemblies as are commonly called Synods or Councils.

II. As magistrates may lawfully call a synod of ministers, and other fit persons, to consult and advise with about matters of religion; so if magistrates be open enemies to the Church, the ministers of Christ, of themselves, by virtue of their office, or they, with other fit persons upon delegation from their Churches, may meet together in such assemblies.*

III. It belongeth to synods and councils ministerially to determine controversies of faith, and cases of conscience; to set down rules and directions for the better ordering of the publick worship of God, and government of His Church; to receive complaints in cases of mal-administration, and authoritatively to determine the same: which decrees and determinations, if consonant to the Word of God, are to be received with reverence and submission, not only for their agreement with the Word, but also for the power whereby they are made, as being an ordinance of God, appointed thereunto in His Word.

IV. All synods or councils since the apostles' times, whether general or particular, may err, and many have erred; therefore they are not to be made the rule of faith or practice, but to be used as an help in both.

V. Synods and councils are to handle or conclude nothing but that which is ecclesiastical; and are not to intermeddle with civil affairs, which concern the commonwealth, unless by way of humble petition, in cases extraordinary; or by way of advice for satisfaction of conscience, if they be thereunto required by the civil magistrate.

---

* From the beginning the Church in Scotland has understood some parts of this section to refer only to churches not settled or constituted in point of government.

APPENDIX TWO

For Further Reading

The Westminster Confession of Faith, chapters 25, 30, also *The Form of Presbyterial Church Government* (Free Presbyterian Publications).

Thomas Witherow, "The Form of the Christian Temple".

James Bannerman, *The Church of Christ* (2 volumes) (Banner of Truth).

R B Kuiper, *The Glorious Body of Christ* (Banner of Truth).

Iain Murray (ed.), *The Reformation of the Church* (Banner of Truth).

Thomas M'Crie, *The Unity of the Church* (Presbyterian Heritage Publications)

R L Dabney, "Prelacy a Blunder", in *Discussions: Evangelical and Theological,* Volume 2 (Banner of Truth).